"Snapping Jaws and Glowing Eyes"

The older sister threw a handful of pebbles into the blackish water. If a crocodile was prowling, this should startle it and scare it away. They had chased off a croc with rocks only a month earlier, so they believed this method was foolproof. But the sisters didn't see the 13-foot female crocodile lurking underwater. The croc had been carefully observing the riverbank and its activity for three days. She knew the sisters were coming. She had smelled them before she had seen them. And now, as the younger sister stepped knee-deep into the river, the big croc began creeping toward her.

CREATURES
THAT CAN
KILL YOU

Marie Noble

 THE TOWNSEND LIBRARY

CREATURES THAT CAN KILL YOU

TP THE TOWNSEND LIBRARY

For more titles in the Townsend Library,
visit our website: **www.townsendpress.com**

Copyright © 2011 by Townsend Press.
Printed in the United States of America

0 9 8 7 6 5 4 3 2 1

Illustrations © 2011 by Hal Taylor

Townsend Press, Inc.
439 Kelley Drive
West Berlin, NJ 08091
permissions@townsendpress.com

ISBN-13: 978-1-59194-268-9
ISBN-10: 1-59194-268-3

Library of Congress Control Number:
2011931327

CONTENTS

Contents

AROUND THE WORLD WITH SNAKES

Preview

Snakes slither through nearly every country on Earth. Most snakes are harmless, but some of them are are anything but. In this chapter, we will travel from India to Australia to Africa. The scariest, the deadliest, and the most feared snakes—they're all here!

AROUND THE WORLD WITH SNAKES

In a rice field in India, a young worker named Abhay stepped carefully around the plants he tended. As always, Abhay listened for any quick rustling through the leaves or, worse yet, a sudden hissing. But as the sky began growing dark with rain clouds, Abhay became careless in his hurry to finish his job. He moved quickly through some taller plants that blocked his view of the ground. Then, just at the edge of the field, Abhay felt something very strange. It was as if a thick cord of rope had been yanked beneath his left foot.

In that same instant, Abhay saw a flash of brown and gold rise up before him—the dreaded Indian cobra. It was not the first time he had seen this terrifying snake. From the time he was a young child, Abhay had often seen these 6- to 10-foot snakes slithering through the village where he lived. They hunted the mice that the village's stores of rice and grain attracted. A cobra was not necessarily dangerous to humans unless it felt threatened or was suddenly surprised. Then it would rear up nearly three feet, flatten out its scaly neck to form a wide "hood," and utter a low, hair-raising hiss. This hiss was the only warning a cobra gave before attacking.

In horror, Abhay now realized he had not only surprised the cobra; he had stepped on it. Everything that happened next seemed to be in slow motion. The long snake sprang up quickly and jerked itself away from under Abhay's foot. Then the cobra reared up and hissed as its dark forked tongue darted in and out. Its black eyes, unblinking and cold, locked onto Abhay's face.

A cobra can lunge more than ten feet. Now it was barely five feet away, and it was poised to strike. Abhay knew his only chance was to remain absolutely still. If a snake no longer felt threatened, sometimes it would just calm down and move on.

Not this time.

Abhay heard the cobra make a strange blowing sound as it suddenly sprang toward him. He reacted by leaping backward and covering his face. A spray of venom spewed out of the cobra's mouth and shot directly toward Abhay's eyes. Abhay had protected his face just in time. If the venom, some of the most poisonous on earth, had hit his eyes, he would have gone blind. Abhay's own uncle had been blinded by a cobra when he was barely 15. It had taken fewer than ten minutes for the venom to destroy his uncle's eyes. The venom had literally burned the eyeballs in their sockets. Nothing had been left but two gaping holes.

Now the cobra backed away. It still stood at attention, but it was no longer poised to strike. It was the break Abhay needed. He backed away slowly until the cobra was more than 20 feet away. Then he sprinted toward the village. Abhay knew that these deadly snakes never chased after humans, but he didn't care. He wasn't about to slow down.

That very same night, a young boy in Abhay's village would not be as lucky as Abhay had been. The boy, named Bai, had gone to bed, as usual, on a grass mat on the floor of his family's small dwelling. Like all the houses in this village, Bai's home was constructed of mud and a loosely thatched roof. Windows had no glass; blankets covered the doorways. For a hungry snake looking for mice, entry into the village's homes was no problem.

In the middle of the night, Bai felt something cold sliding across his cheek. Still half asleep, he reached up to brush it away. Suddenly, Bai felt something puncture his wrist. Then a loud rustling and swishing filled the room. Bai sat up and grabbed a lantern. In its dim light, he saw a long black and yellow snake slithering out the door.

"Mother! Come quickly!" Bai shouted. "I have been bitten by a snake!"

Bai's mother rushed outside to see if she could see what kind of snake had bitten her son.

"The snake climbed up the mud wall of the house and crawled in a hole in the brickwork," Bai's mother recalled. "I knew this was terrible. I recognized that snake at once."

Bai had been bitten by a krait, a snake whose venom is twice as deadly as a cobra's. Though the villagers went into the woods to gather herbs for a paste to put on the bite, it would not do any good. Within an hour, Bai's breathing became a heavy wheeze. Next, his entire body turned a sickening yellow, and his bitten arm swelled to three times its normal size. Just before dawn, he turned to his mother.

"I know you will not be able to save me now," he whispered. "Goodbye."

By the time the first rays of sun crept into the village, Bai was dead.

It may seem shocking to think that in the very same evening, two people from the same small village in India were attacked by deadly snakes. However, the facts about deaths by snakebite in India are even more appalling. It is estimated that somewhere between 10,000 and 30,000 Indians die *every year* after being bitten by cobras, kraits, and vipers. It is hard to know exact numbers, since many deaths are not reported. And of the thousands more who are bitten and don't die, the effects of the venom are often crippling. Cobra venom is often compared to battery acid. It eats away at skin and muscle and turns limbs black and lifeless.

Still, to many living in rural India, snakes are simply an everyday fact of life. Cobras and kraits are, in some areas, nearly as common as squirrels or chipmunks in many parts of the United States. But the high numbers of snakebites are not a result of Indian people being careless or unconcerned about snakes. Most of these victims live in poverty. They work barefoot in fields and live in poorly built homes. Making matters worse, many of these Indians have no access to the kind of medical care needed when bitten by a snake.

"We say our goodbyes when the cobra has made its mark," one villager explained.

Nearly 5,000 miles away from India, on the continent of Australia, there are snakes that put the cobra to shame. Around the world, there are more than 3,000 different kinds of snakes, but less than ten percent of them are poisonous. However, in Australia, of the 130 different snakes that live there, more than half are deadly—very deadly.

Consider a snake that reaches ten feet in length and carries around enough venom to kill 60 to 100 grown men. This is the Australian inland taipan. The taipan has often been labeled the most poisonous snake on earth. Its half-inch fangs (huge for a snake!) are curved so that when it bites, it holds on. Even a quick nip from a taipan can deliver enough venom to kill. A milligram of taipan venom is enough to kill a dozen people. How much is a milligram? Imagine crushing a peanut into seven hundred pieces. Then take just one of those pieces. That is a milligram.

And like many Australian snakes, the taipan is unusually vicious when cornered. Most snakes, even the cobra, will retreat after striking a victim. But the taipan seems to have a pretty bad temper. It will strike and bite over and over again, refusing to back down or move away. And once its venom mixes with human blood, a terrible thing happens. The toxins in a taipan's bite turn blood into a kind of thick mud that can't move through veins. No blood flow means a quick and very painful death, usually in less than an hour.

But there's good news when it comes to the taipan. There is no record of an inland taipan ever having killed a human. The reason is simple. Very few people live or visit the remote area in central Australia where most inland taipans live. It is a hot, rocky area that extends for hundreds of miles. Scientists have captured and studied inland taipans, and, in fact, a few scientists have been bitten. But these researchers have always had a supply of anti-venom close by.

Sadly, a young man who was interested in the coastal taipans, which live near the ocean, was not as fortunate.

"I just wanted to collect a specimen."

These were some of the last words that 20-year-old Kevin Budden ever spoke. Budden had always been fascinated by the dangerous taipans, but he had never captured one for his snake collection. Once in a very great while, there were reports of people being bitten by these coastal taipans, the close cousins of the inland taipans. No one ever survived. This fact only increased

Budden's curiosity. Finally, in the summer of 1950, Budden followed up on some news of taipan sightings along the Australian coast near Queensland.

Budden searched for days with no luck. Then, one morning, as he wandered through rubble piled up near a construction site, he heard the loud squeal of a rat. Knowing that snakes eat rats, Budden quietly walked to the source of the squeal. Then, lifting an old piece of plastic, he uncovered a 5-foot-long brown snake with the rat halfway in its mouth. In a flash, Budden placed his foot over the snake's neck, forcing it to spit out the rat. Then he reached down and grasped the snake tightly around its throat with both hands so that it couldn't bite him.

Now Budden was in a bind. He couldn't reach the specimen bag lying nearby, and even if he could, he didn't have a free hand. His only option was to walk to the main road. Once there, Budden hoped someone would give him a ride back to the house of a friend who was also a snake collector. It's hard to believe that anyone would stop to give a ride to a stranger holding a 5-foot snake, but someone did.

"What have you got there?" the driver asked somewhat casually, assuming this was just some kid who liked to collect harmless snakes.

"Not sure," Budden responded. "But I'm sure hoping it's a taipan."

The driver slammed on the brakes and shouted for Budden to get out of his car immediately. But Budden pleaded with him.

"It's for research," he added, exaggerating just a bit. "And I have a firm grip on it. There's no way it can hurt us."

Reluctantly (and very quickly), the driver drove Budden the ten miles to his friend's house. By the time Budden got out of the car, his arms were shaking with nervousness and fatigue. His hands were covered with the snake's saliva and, possibly, venom. But he had succeeded. His friend confirmed that what Budden held was indeed a coastal taipan.

"Quick," Budden said excitedly. "Get a specimen bag. I can't hold on much longer."

Just as his friend returned with the thick sack, Budden's grip failed. Like the quick snap of a whip, the taipan sunk its fangs repeatedly into Budden's left hand. Budden looked at his friend in terror. He knew all too well what the bite of a taipan meant. Even so, as the two men waited for the ambulance, Budden made his friend promise that he would not kill the snake. After all, it had only done what any frightened and cornered snake would do. It wasn't the taipan's fault.

In spite of the best medical care and doses of anti-venom, the multiple bites had taken their toll. There was just too much poison in Budden's body. Little by little, his blood thickened, and his organs shut down. By the next morning, he was dead—one of the few recorded victims of the world's most venomous snake.

If India has the deadliest snakes and Australia has the most poisonous, Africa might win the prize for having the most feared snake. What makes one snake more frightening than another? It's hard to say, but some Africans will tell you that it has to do with a snake's size, speed, intelligence, and appearance. And East and South Africa's black mamba snake gets top marks in all these areas.

It's certainly true that the black mamba is a scary-looking serpent. Reaching lengths of nearly 15 feet, this slender snake has a thick coffin-shaped head and large black unblinking eyes. Its body is gray, not black, but it came by its name because of its mouth. When the black mamba feels threatened, it opens its unusually large jaws to reveal a jet-black tongue and mouth. Some say that the hiss that comes out of this inky mouth sounds like low thunder from a dark cloud.

Adding to this snake's fearsome appearance is

its ability to "stand up" nearly four feet high and move quickly through the grasses in the African savannah. The black mamba stands to get a better view of the mice and other rodents it hunts. But to the Africans who have suddenly come face to face with the mamba, it seems as though the snake is looking for humans instead.

And it's definitely true that the black mamba is fast. Most snakes can't move much faster than 5 to 7 miles an hour. The black mamba, however, has been known to cruise along at speeds of nearly 12 miles an hour. This makes it the fastest snake on earth. While the mamba usually uses its speed to catch prey or flee from humans, it has been known, on very rare occasions, to rush after those who accidentally corner it. But these extremely rare instances of mambas chasing down humans have been exaggerated again and again in stories. Over time, a great deal of the fear connected to the mamba has grown out of myths about this snake.

It is most certainly *not* true that the black mamba plots revenge on humans who take over its land. Or that it bites its tail to make a loop so that it can roll quickly down a hill, and then flattens itself into an arrow shape that speeds through the air at 30 miles an hour. It does not create whirlwinds that can be seen from half a

mile away. Nor does it ambush people by curl-
ing into a circle around car tires, waiting to bite
the driver as soon as he or she steps out of the
car. And while some Africans swear that the black
mamba waits in treetops, plotting to jump onto
the heads of unsuspecting passersby, this is pretty
unlikely. The mamba is mostly a ground dweller
and generally avoids trees.

The bottom line is that the black mamba is
simply a very fast and poisonous snake with a
scary face. Like any dangerous snake in any corner of the world, the mamba would heartily prefer to avoid humans altogether. It will go to great
lengths to stay out of people's way. However,
when it is forced into contact, it will fight back.
Such behavior is expected of any wild creature,
but when the creature is as creepy-looking as a
snake (No legs! No eyelids! Forked tongue!), its
natural behavior is looked at as evil and super-
dangerous.

But truth be told, we would sorely miss
snakes, even the dreaded mamba, if they weren't
around. Snakes keep the mice and rat population
from overwhelming many parts of the world.
Millions more people have been killed by diseases
carried by rats and mice than will ever be killed
by snakes. Furthermore, many non-poisonous
snakes are a main source of food for birds and

other small mammals. Take away snakes, and the entire food chain would begin to break down.

"Some people think that the only good snake is a dead snake, and that's really too bad," a snake expert (known as a "herpetologist") once explained. "If all the snakes in the world were suddenly dead, humans would not be far behind them."

GRIZZLY!

Preview

When Sarah Mullen decided
to take a short hike along
a familiar trail, she never
imagined the nightmare
that was waiting for her.
Up ahead, in a field, a huge
grizzly quietly hunted for
berries. But when Sarah
accidentally surprised the
bear, the calm was shattered.
Suddenly, 700 pounds
of claws and fangs came
rushing toward Sarah at
30 miles an hour.

GRIZZLY!

Enter the world of the grizzly bear.

This big brown bear, in spite of its fierce reputation and looks, usually goes out of its way to avoid trouble. It doesn't particularly like to fight. Those huge claws? They're mostly for digging up roots and wild vegetables. The sharp teeth? Those come in handy for munching the rodents and other mammals the grizzly very occasionally hunts. In fact, the grizzly is probably happiest sitting in a warm berry patch on a summer morning, eating wild strawberries and napping. More than 90 percent of a grizzly bear's diet is made up of insects, fish, nuts, berries, and roots. It rarely hunts large animals, and it never hunts humans.

A full-grown grizzly stands nearly 8 feet tall and can weigh 1,000 pounds. However, the grizzly's size has more to do with the way it lives than with being equipped to kill. Every year, as fall fades into winter, the grizzly bear waits for the first big snowfall. Then it finds a small den or cave high on a mountainside. Using its huge claws, it digs further in, curls up, and sleeps for the next five months or more. Obviously, any creature that snoozes that long without a meal has got to pack on a lot of weight to get through the winter. It is estimated that many grizzlies gain 400 pounds before retiring to their dens. That's a lot of strawberries and roots.

In the spring, the grizzly bear emerges from its cave very hungry and, understandably, a little irritable and short-tempered. This is one of the two most dangerous times for humans to cross paths with grizzlies. The territory a grizzly covers when searching for food can be 150 to 500 miles. In places like Alaska, Yellowstone Park in Wyoming, and parks and recreation centers in western Canada, a grizzly bear's territory often extends into areas where people live. And a ravenous bear will not think twice about going after people's garbage or, really, any food it can get to. Though a grizzly's eyesight is poor, its sense of smell is amazing. From a half mile away, a grizzly can smell an old cantaloupe rind someone threw out two days earlier. And after a half year without food, a grizzly bear will be determined to get that rind.

The grizzly is mostly a loner. It does not travel in groups, and it generally does not like the company of other bears. The exception to this behavior, of course, occurs during the mating season in June. During this time, male grizzlies will pick a mate and follow her around for a week or more. Sometimes this leads to terrifically brutal fights between male grizzlies that have set their sights on the same female. A female may watch the fights from a distance, deciding whether or not she will mate with the winner. It is not uncommon for the female to turn down the winner with a swat and a growl.

However, once all the dust settles, a pregnant female grizzly will give birth 180 to 250 days later—right in the middle of hibernation! She wakes up briefly, gives birth to two to four cubs, cleans and feeds them, and returns to her slumber. Though the cubs are born blind and weigh barely one pound, they will grow extremely quickly. They nurse on their mother's rich milk (30 percent fat) and sleep close to her until early spring. When spring's warmth begins to creep into the den, the mother bear, known as a sow, will lead her cubs out into the sunlight for the first time.

From this first walk in the sun until three years later, when the cubs are grown, a mother grizzly is a terribly dangerous force to be reckoned with. It has been said that there is no creature on earth more protective of its young than a female grizzly. She will often perceive the mere presence of another animal as a threat to her cubs. Wolves and mountain lions have been known to hunt young cubs, although they would never attack a full-grown grizzly. There is only one animal on earth that truly threatens the grizzly—man. It is not surprising, then, that mother grizzly bears become particularly ferocious when they catch the scent of a human, *any* human, wandering near their young.

Here's what can happen when a young woman enters the world of the grizzly bear.

Sarah Mullen had had the perfect long weekend. She had spent four days with her boyfriend and friends in Yellowstone National Park. The group had hiked, ridden horses, and camped out. It was a kind of homecoming for Sarah. She had worked for years in the park on a trail crew, clearing and maintaining trails for hikers. But now her new job had taken her four hours away from Yellowstone. For nearly half a year, she had been missing the wilderness she knew so well.

"Don't you want to ride a horse back to town?" her boyfriend, Pete, asked Sarah when the weekend was over. It was time to return to the lot where the cars were parked.

"I think I'll walk," Sarah replied. "It'll be nice to have one last hike."

It was only five miles back into town, and Sarah was very familiar with this particular trail. It was like an old friend, and she thought she'd spend some time alone with it. That morning, she left early so that those on horseback would be behind her. They would all meet at the parking lot at the same time.

"Sure you'll be all right?" Pete asked with a grin, knowing that Sarah would be fine.

"Yeah," Sarah said. "Unless I get attacked by a bear."

Pete gave her a funny look. "Well, don't say that!" he said anxiously.

"Oh, come on. You know I'm joking!" Sarah said with a laugh. "It's only five miles."

It was a spectacular morning for a walk. Spring had finally hit Yellowstone full blast, and flowers and plants were in bloom everywhere. Sarah made her way along the trail, listening to all the busy sounds of the birds and animals across the mountainside. Then a strange sound kept getting closer and closer. It was a sort of scratching and snorting. Just as Sarah rounded a corner, she saw what it was—a large bear digging up new spring plants to eat.

"I thought, 'Oh no,' and I started backing up," Sarah remembered. "I was moving backward, looking for a tree to climb."

The bear had not yet seen Sarah. Sarah was not panicking, because she assumed this was a black bear. She had often seen black bears near the trails, and they generally just ambled off when humans got too close. But Sarah knew it was best to play it safe, look for a tree, and not startle the bear. At that moment, however, several terrible things happened all at once.

"Weeeeeee!!!"

Sarah heard a high-pitched squeal, and then three small heads popped up above the grass. Bear cubs! One of the cubs had spotted Sarah and was now warning its mother with a cry. The mother stood up, sniffing the air and squinting. Immediately, Sarah froze in terror. This was no mild-mannered black bear—this was a grizzly. And now it was staring straight into Sarah's face.

In an instant, the mother bear began her charge. A grown grizzly can run in short spurts at nearly 30 miles per hour, and an angry sow can cover one hundred yards in barely 7 seconds. This sow was about 80 yards away.

She's bluffing, Sarah thought desperately. Sometimes grizzlies will fake a charge in hopes that the threatening visitor will just leave. But this was no bluff. The bear was coming straight at Sarah with its large yellowish fangs now bared. Sarah had maybe two seconds to come up with a plan. She threw down a water bottle, hoping to distract the grizzly, but the big bear did not even glance at it. Sarah's last hope was to play dead, but before she had a chance to drop to the ground, the grizzly was on her.

First, the grizzly sank her teeth into Sarah's face. Then the bear bit her shoulder and ribcage. Seven rib bones snapped, one after the other. In one of those weird moments of disconnection that people sometimes have in life-and-death situations, Sarah remembers thinking how loud the cracking of her bones was. However, the loudest crunch came when the grizzly opened her mouth wide and grabbed Sarah's skull in her jaws. Teeth punctured the back of Sarah's head all the way around to her right eye. Then, like a dog might pick up a toy and shake it, the bear lifted

Sarah off the ground in its teeth and gave her a mighty shake. Sarah recalled being flung through the air and slammed into a tree. Though both her eyes were full of blood, she could still make out the menacing dark form of the grizzly moving toward her again.

It was at that point that Sarah began screaming. She screamed in anger, terror, and pain. She screamed to God to help her. She screamed at the bear, calling the sow every foul name she could think of. And it worked. The grizzly stopped just in front of Sarah, lifted its head to sniff the air, snorted once, and walked away. The entire attack had taken around 10 seconds.

"I don't know why she left. That's the million-dollar question," Sarah later commented. "Did she leave because I was down on the ground and no longer a threat to her cubs? Did she leave because I screamed so loudly?"

It's not uncommon for grizzlies to suddenly stop their attack once they sense that what they're attacking has become helpless. And now, Sarah was beyond helpless. She knew that if she didn't get aid soon, she would bleed to death. She managed to reach a pack of Kleenex that had fallen out of her pack. Now she attempted to stuff tissues into the holes in her head to stop the bleeding. She spoke out loud to herself to keep from losing consciousness. And she prayed that Pete and the others, who were behind her on horseback, would reach her before she died.

Sarah was unusually lucky. Her friends did get to her before she lost too much blood. While one friend stayed with her and helped cover her wounds, Pete rushed to town to get paramedics. Sarah remembered that while she waited, flies came in swarms, attracted by the smell of blood. Even a hummingbird, drawn to the pools of bright red on the ground, flew in to take a look.

It would take weeks of hospitalization and some very creative surgery to piece Sarah back together. One of her eyes had fallen out of its socket and had to be re-fitted. The bones around her eyes had to be wired to her nose. Hundreds of stitches covered her body. Her ribs were so badly cracked that they would never heal completely. This made it difficult for Sarah to hug her friends and impossible for her to ever carry a backpack again. And yet, to this day, Sarah feels no hatred or anger toward her attacker. In fact, her first request when rescuers reached her was that the bear not be killed. Often the National Park Service will hunt down bears that have attacked people. But Sarah insisted that this grizzly was probably not dangerous and was not to be blamed for what happened.

"I made the mistake of moving quickly and quietly and alone through grizzly country," she later explained. "The bear was only trying to protect its children, and who could blame any mother for that?"

Sarah Mullen's surviving a grizzly attack may seem like a miracle, but it's really not that unusual. With its five-inch claws and ability to take an entire human head into its mouth, a determined grizzly would have little problem tearing a person apart in seconds. Most grizzlies outweigh humans by 500 or more pounds, and their paws sometimes measure a foot across. A simple, well-placed swat could kill a man. Yet, more often than not, a grizzly will walk away from its victim while the person is still alive. Why?

For one thing, except in extremely rare cases, a grizzly is not interested in eating or killing a human. It simply wants to give a warning, to let the intruder know that he or she is not welcome in its territory or near its cubs. This is why, more often than not, a grizzly will merely bluff an attack. It will dash forward once or twice, bare its teeth, and stand up to show its size. It may even take a swipe at the air right in front of a cornered person's face. But, in the end, it will leave without inflicting any pain.

"When a grizzly bluffs, the best thing to do is what you might do with a threatening dog," one experienced ranger at Yellowstone explained. "Speak softly, and don't make any sudden movements. The last thing you want to do is turn around and run. That will only guarantee being chased."

It's not just coincidence that a grizzly acts somewhat like a dog—the two are ancient cousins. Thirty-eight million years ago, dogs and bears looked very much alike. Today, bears still resemble dogs in their snouts, teeth, and paws. More importantly, they share similar brains. However, most scientists agree that a grizzly bear appears to be far smarter than a dog.

"They are perhaps as intelligent as the great apes. They have a good sense of their surroundings, their threats, and their enemies," a bear specialist claimed. "Considering what humans have done to them, it's not surprising that they dislike us. Actually, it's pretty amazing that they don't kill every human they can get their paws on."

What humans have done to grizzlies is to drive them nearly to extinction in the lower 48 United States. For many centuries, Native Americans had honored and respected the grizzly for its awesome power, but that all changed by the twentieth century.

"A grizzly has no more chance against a man with a modern rifle than a fly has against a sledgehammer," an Arctic and Alaskan explorer once noted.

And for many years grizzlies were killed for their fur, their skulls, and often just because they looked so fierce. To some people, it seemed like a good idea to get rid of them. Over the past 100 years or so, humans have reduced the grizzly population in the lower 48 states from 50,000 to 1,000. Grizzly bears used to roam forests and mountains as far south as Texas, but now they can be found in only a few states. Thankfully, grizzlies still thrive in Alaska and parts of Canada, and laws have been put in place to protect them.

Grizzlies, and all bears in general, tend to be thought of in extremes. They are seen as either ferocious killers or Winnie-the-Pooh teddy bears. In fact, they are neither. They are naturally peaceful, wise creatures that just want to have the space and food they need. They prefer to be left alone and would rather avoid conflict. However, they are very protective of both their cubs and the food they need to survive. They will fight anyone or anything that threatens either.

It is, then, not all that surprising that the majority of people who have been attacked by grizzlies don't blame the bear. And, like Sarah Mullen, they don't want the bear killed.

"When you think about it," said one survivor who needed 310 stitches, "grizzlies and humans are a lot alike. Maybe more alike than we'd like to admit."

ANCIENT, AWESOME PREDATOR: THE SHARK

Preview

Near a popular beach in New Jersey, a long, dark shadow is spotted moving through the water. Suddenly screams fill the air, and the ocean water turns red with a swimmer's blood. Only days later, the shadow appears again, bringing more death and fear. And now, the dark form swims toward three boys playing in an ocean inlet. Frantic shouts ring out: "Watch out! Shark!"

ANCIENT, AWESOME PREDATOR: THE SHARK

Are you afraid to swim in the ocean because of sharks? Then here are some facts to consider: Your chances of getting killed by a shark are one in 265 million. You are a thousand times more likely to drown while you are taking that swim than you are to suffer a shark bite. Your chances of dying due to an airplane part falling out of the sky are nearly ten times greater than your chances of dying from a shark attack. And as one shark expert noted, "More people are killed by pigs on farms in Iowa every year in the United States than by sharks."

Still, many of us have a deep fear of these silent, steely-eyed predators. And even though sharks are not really a serious threat to humans, they do have some pretty scary characteristics. For example, a shark can smell a single droplet of blood in a million gallons of ocean water. It can sense the smallest movements in the water more than a mile away. Sharkskin is so rough that it can cut and even slice on contact. Before sandpaper was invented, people often used sharkskin to smooth wood and rock. It was also wrapped around sword handles to keep swords from sliding out of sweaty hands.

Even more dangerous than the shark's skin are its teeth. It is, perhaps, the shark's impressive display of knife-pointed and razor-edged teeth that frightens us the most. About four dozen teeth line the shark's mouth. That may not seem like a lot for the size of a shark's jaw. However, seven rows of replacement teeth behind each tooth make the shark's mouth resemble a slicing and dicing machine. Within 24 hours of losing a tooth, a new tooth will move forward to take its place. It is estimated that the average shark will go through 30,000 teeth in its lifetime! And as a shark gets older, its teeth get bigger and bigger. Not surprisingly, the oldest and biggest sharks look the most terrifying when they open their mouths.

Sharks live all over the world, and for thousands of years, humans have been fascinated by these big fish. In prehistoric times, men combed beaches, looking for shark teeth to use for tools, weapons, and jewelry. Many ancient cultures believed that sharks were really gods who ruled the underwater world of the sea. Pearl divers would often tattoo themselves with images of sharks. They hoped that this show of respect would please the shark gods. And while people knew that the shark's bite could inflict some pretty hefty damage, the shark was typically admired more than it was feared.

In the United States, even as recently as the early 1900s, sharks were not really considered dangerous. Perhaps on a rare occasion, a fisherman might die from a shark bite. Once in a very great while, a swimmer might disappear, possibly the result of an accidental run-in with a shark. But no one particularly worried about sharks. No one thought that sharks would intentionally come after humans any more than, say, a jellyfish or stingray would. Then, in July 1916, something happened that would begin to change people's view of sharks.

The summer of 1916 had been brutally hot in the northeastern United States. Making things worse, the deadly disease called polio had spread from New York to New Jersey. Because many believed that polio was caused by hot and humid conditions, thousands of people flocked to the nearby beaches, where the air was cooler. One of these thousands was a young man named Charles Vansant. Vansant was handsome and energetic and eagerly looking forward to a promising future. He had just graduated from the University of Pennsylvania, and he was beginning a new job with a law firm in the fall.

Late in the afternoon of July 1, Vansant rushed out onto the sands of Beach Haven along the New Jersey shoreline. It had been a long, hot train ride to the little seashore resort, and now Vansant was ready for a swim before dinner. His excitement attracted a golden retriever; it splashed in the surf with Vansant and swam out a bit with him. Suddenly, the dog changed its mind and swam quickly back to the shore. Vansant whistled and called for the dog, but it refused to return to the water. At that same moment, several people on the beach noticed a long dark shape beneath the water, moving toward Vansant.

"Only seconds later, the young man began shouting and splashing in the water," one observer recalled. "I think everyone thought he was still trying to get the dog to come back to him."

The shouting drew the attention of the

lifeguard, who was a friend of Vansant's named Alex Ott. As the shouts became shrieks, Ott raced toward the water. Something was dragging his friend beneath the surface, and now the water surrounding Vansant was turning crimson. Somehow, Vansant managed to struggle to waist-deep water as Ott rushed to grab his hands and pull him to safety. From the nearby boardwalk, onlookers swore they could see a nine-foot shark still attached to Vansant's thigh. The shark held on until the water was barely two feet deep. Finally, as the water got too shallow, the large shark released its grip and swam off.

Once on the beach, Ott could tell right away that his friend was dying. Nearly all the flesh along the back of Vansant's left thigh had been torn away, and the bone was exposed. The front of his right leg looked just as bad. Major arteries had been cut, and now Vansant was bleeding to death. Although Ott did what he could to stop the blood, Vansant was dead within an hour.

The next day, newspapers did not have much to say about the attack. *The New York Times* mentioned it briefly on page 18, but referred to the shark as "a fish." A notice to vacationers at Beach Haven announced: "Bathers need have no fear of sharks. Fish experts have declared that the one that killed the swimmer may have been after the dog." Within days, the beach was as crowded as ever. After all, this was the first shark fatality ever recorded on the east coast of the United States. No one was too concerned.

Then, a week later and only 20 miles north of Beach Haven, another young man went for a fateful swim. Just as he swam out beyond the lifelines that marked the swimming area, he was pulled underwater. Then he was pushed violently up into the air. As he screamed and crashed back into the sea, he attracted the attention of a woman on the beach.

"Somebody help that man in the red canoe!" she shouted. "He's fallen out!"

But the red canoe she thought she saw was really the man's blood gushing into the water. A rescue boat rushed out to help the young man.

"We saw his arm waving out of the water, so we pulled him up," a rescuer remembered. "We were surprised that he seemed so light."

When the man was hauled into the boat, it became clear why he was so light: the bottom half of his body was missing.

Five days later, a retired sea captain stood on a bridge overlooking a bay not far from Beach Haven. Connected to the bay was a narrow inlet called Matawan Creek. As he watched the fish swimming in the creek, he spotted something that he could hardly believe was real. A ten-foot shark was cruising quickly up the creek and toward the docks and boats that lined it. In all his years of fishing and watching the water, the captain had never seen a big shark enter Matawan Creek.

The captain ran toward the small town on the creek to warn the people, but he was mostly ignored. A huge shark in such a narrow creek? Impossible! Most of the townspeople assumed that the captain had paid a little too much attention to the recent shark attacks. Perhaps he had been drinking. Now, they thought, he was imagining things and just stirring up fear. Meanwhile, three young boys jumped off a dock and into the creek for a cool afternoon swim.

"What is *that*?" one of the boys asked his friend, pointing to a long, dark shape moving through the water toward their other friend, Lester Stillwell. Just as it reached Lester, a dark fin cut through the water's surface.

"Lester! Watch out!" the two boys shouted. But it was too late. There was a mighty splash and one quick scream. Then Lester vanished. All the boys could see was a spreading sheen of blood on the water. Terrified, the two other boys scrambled out of the creek and ran into town, screaming, "Shark! Shark!" Soon, a crowd of men from the town was rushing to the creek, armed with hooks and poles, to search for Lester's body. They knew the boy would not be found alive.

They also took a long wire net to stretch across the creek so that Lester's corpse would not float back out to sea when the tide changed. Unfortunately, there was one serious problem with the net.

"Once we stretched the wire net across, the shark couldn't get out either," one man remembered. "Somehow, nobody had thought about that. I guess we all assumed it had already left."

But the shark was still quite close to the dock, swimming close to where it had left Lester's body. For hours, several men searched in boats, and three very brave men actually swam around, diving to the bottom of the creek to look for the boy. Suddenly, there was a loud screech from Stan Fisher, one of the swimmers. Horrified onlookers watched as Fisher battled the shark. It clamped its jaws around Fisher's leg and tried to drag him under. In Fisher's arms were what remained of Lester Stillwell. Clearly, the shark did not want to give up its kill. Somehow, Fisher got away from the shark and dragged himself to the dock.

"I knew it was all over with me when I felt the shark's grip on my thigh," Fisher would later say in the hospital. "It was an awful feeling. I can't explain it. Anyhow, I did my duty."

Those were Fisher's final words. His left leg had been nearly torn off, and he died one hour later from blood loss.

Four people had been killed in less than two weeks by what had become known as the "Matawan Beast." In a rage, people dynamited Matawan Creek and threw spears and knives at any large dark object seen moving in the water. Some men headed out on fishing boats with guns and explosives. Suddenly, all sharks were the enemy, and people couldn't kill them quickly enough. From Maine to New Jersey, numerous people claimed to have caught the killer shark. These claims were finally put to rest when a New York fisherman caught a ten-foot great white shark. When the shark was cut open, its stomach contained "fifteen pounds of human flesh and bone, including the shin bone of a boy, and a human rib." Finally, the terrible "Summer of the Shark" had ended.

That summer of 1916, however, marked the beginning of Americans' fascination with sharks—and their overblown fear of them. Sharks had previously been thought of as just another sea creature to avoid. Now they were seen as evil and murderous monsters. The word "shark" became a synonym for anyone or anything that was sneaky, dangerous, fierce, or aggressive. The shark attacks of 1916 were exceedingly unusual. Still, many people began to believe that all sharks hunt humans and pose a real threat to them.

In fact, nothing could be further from the truth. Most sharks are quite shy, preferring to remain as far away from humans as possible. Contrary to the idea that sharks are "killing machines" that constantly hunt and eat anything they can find, sharks eat only when they are hungry. What's more, their bodies are so efficient at storing food that they can often go for weeks between meals. Their preferred meals are fish or seals, which are very high in oil and fat content. Human flesh is not appealing to them at all.

Why, then, do sharks ever attack humans? Most scientists agree that shark attacks usually result from either simple cases of "mistaken identity" or just plain old curiosity. Surfboards, kayaks, and divers in wetsuits might all look like seals to a hungry shark. Most sharks will take a quick bite, realize their mistake, and swim off. Of course, the quick bite of a great white shark can kill a human, so these test bites become translated as "deadly shark attacks." In turn, this continues to fan the flame of shark fear.

And on rare occasions, a shark may sink its

teeth into a human just to see what we are. Unlike most other predators, a shark does not have claws and paws it can use to investigate something. Sharks figure things out by biting, sensing whether or not what they've bitten is edible, and then either taking another nip or swimming away. This habit has led sharks to take bites out of everything from boat propellers to license plates to humans. Clearly, humans are something a shark is eager to spit back out. Only about 60 people worldwide are bitten by sharks every year, and of these 60, sharks typically release 50. It is extremely rare for a shark to seek out human flesh.

Even so, the myths and the exaggerated fear of sharks persist. This fear was given a big boost during World War II. When the American warship *Indianapolis* was sunk by a Japanese submarine, hundreds of American sailors were eaten by deep sea whitetip sharks. Of the 1,200 men on board the *Indianapolis*, 880 made it into the Pacific Ocean alive as their ship sank. But many of these sailors were wounded, bleeding, and burned. Sharks, attracted by the smell of blood, swarmed around the sailors.

"One by one, sharks began picking off the men on the outside of the clustered groups," one surviving sailor remembered. "Agonizing screams filled the air day and night. Blood mixed with the fuel oil. . . . It was a terror-filled ordeal—never knowing if you'd be the next victim."

For five days, men remained stranded in the ocean, awaiting rescue. During this time, hundreds died from injuries, exposure, and thirst. Without a doubt, whitetip sharks added both misery and panic to this wait. However, the majority of deaths were not caused by sharks. Still, dozens, and possibly hundreds, of corpses were dragged away and mangled by the whitetips. This led experts to agree that the sinking of the *Indianapolis* resulted in the most shark attacks on humans ever recorded. In the end, only 316 of the 880 soldiers who had survived the submarine attack ended up surviving the terrifying wait in the water.

"The Pacific Ocean is infested with killer sharks!"

"Sharks are the most dangerous creatures on earth!"

"Sharks must be killed!"

A wave of alarm and fear spread throughout the United States following the *Indianapolis* disaster. It didn't really matter that sharks were not to blame for most of the deaths—it was still what many people chose to believe. Stories and films that exaggerated the shark attacks on the sailors were all the sensation. Shark hunts grew more and more popular as the myths that portrayed sharks as enemies became more widespread.

Hatred and fear of sharks may have reached its peak 30 years after the sinking of the *Indianapolis*. When the novel *Jaws*, by author Peter Benchley, was released in 1974, it was a tremendous bestseller that soon became a blockbuster movie. In fact, Benchley based his story on those events that had taken place at Beach Haven and Matawan Creek so many years earlier. The book and movie starred a fictional monster of a shark. This shark appeared to want to wage war on humans and spend every minute of its life tracking and hunting human blood. This shark was so intelligent that it even plotted attacks for revenge.

In response to the book and movie, many people completely overreacted by waging a cruel and needless war on sharks. In particular, the great white shark (the star of *Jaws*) was targeted and killed by the thousands. A shark that had already been declining in numbers was now becoming truly endangered. By the 1980s, it was estimated that for every human being killed by a shark, *two million* sharks were slaughtered for sport, skin, meat, and fins.

Thankfully, laws and restrictions have now been put into place to help save these ancient kings of the ocean. Today it is illegal to kill great whites in many areas of the world, including parts of the United States. Some years after the success of *Jaws*, Peter Benchley said he truly regretted the negative reactions toward sharks that his book had created. He felt guilty and responsible. As a result, he would dedicate the rest of his life to helping save sharks and to changing the way people felt about them.

"Considering the knowledge gathered about sharks in the last 25 years, I couldn't possibly write *Jaws* today," Benchley said in 2000. "Back then, it was generally accepted that great whites ate people by choice. Now we know that almost every attack on a human is an accident. The shark simply mistakes the human for its normal prey."

THE BIG CATS

Preview

More than one hundred
years ago, in a desolate part
of Africa, something terrible
was happening. Night after
night, two young lions
crept into a camp of railway
workers, seized men by
their necks or feet, and
dragged them away. The
next day, all that could be
found were the bones and
the skulls of the victims.
Why were these lions
hunting human flesh?
And what could be
done to stop them?

THE BIG CATS

"**B**eware, brothers! The devil is coming!"

The shouts of warning passed from tent to tent. It was the middle of the night in a remote part of East Kenya. A sudden silence had instantly terrified the hundreds of men camped near the Tsavo River. Silence was usually welcome out in this wild area. The long nights were often interrupted by the growls, calls, and shrieks of the animals that lived out on the grasslands known as the savannah. But now the utter stillness sent a wave of dread.

The men were railway workers from India, hired by the British to build a bridge over the river. Now they lay on their cots shaking. Some held knives in their hands, while others clasped their hands in prayer. Somewhere in the pitch-black night, not too far away, two killer lions were creeping toward the tents. They would take their time, but they would already have chosen their victim. Hidden behind tall grasses and rocks, the lions had spent the cool evening observing the men. Perhaps they had spotted an injured worker, a man who was smaller than the others, or a worker who appeared sick or weak.

Now, in the dead of night, the young lions moved in for the kill.

For nearly half a year, the work crew had lived in fear. The lions might go a week or more without an attack, but when the men heard the distant roaring at sunset, they knew they were in for a night of terror.

"In the whole of my life, I have never experienced anything more nerve-shaking than to hear the deep roars of these dreadful monsters growing gradually nearer and nearer," the chief engineer of the project, John Patterson, later wrote, "and to know that one of us was doomed to be their victim before morning dawned."

When the two big cats were just outside the camp, the roaring stopped. They began moving soundlessly toward their victim. And now, many of the men virtually held their breath, waiting to hear the screams they knew would come.

The workers had tried everything to ward off the lions, but this was 1898 in the wilds of East Africa. The tents were wide open, guns were scarce, and the only source of light was campfires or burning torches. A long barrier fence made of thorns had been constructed, but the lions had had no problem leaping right over it. When the workers realized that the lions dragged victims off by their feet, the men began sleeping in a circle with their feet facing in. In response, the lions began grabbing men around the head and neck.

The two lions, now referred to as the "Man-eaters of Tsavo," were brothers. They were still too young to have grown manes, but they were old enough to be skilled hunters of human flesh. For nearly a year, the lions preyed on the Indian railroad workers and nearby Kenyan villagers. John Patterson estimated that within 9 months, the cats ate 135 people. In desperation, traps were set; guns were fired blindly into the darkness; and daytime hunts, led by Patterson, became weekly events. Nothing worked. Somehow, the cats always mysteriously slipped away into the night. During the day, the young lions remained hidden.

As the lions became more comfortable with hunting humans, they became bolder. At first, one cat had waited in the bushes while the other cat made the attack and dragged a body back to feast on. Now, both lions were attacking at once. Terrified screams from two different tents often shattered the night. And while the lions had previously hauled the bodies a quarter of a mile or more from the work camp, they now began eating barely 100 yards away from the tents.

"I have a very vivid recollection of one particular night," John Patterson wrote. "The brutes had brought a man close to my camp to devour. I could plainly hear them crunching the bones, and their dreadful purring filled the air and rang in my ears for days afterwards."

In the mornings, Patterson had the gruesome job of tracking down the remains of the lions' victims. Usually, a trail of blood led to the spot where the cats had eaten. This trail was the result of the big cats' method of killing quickly: by biting the victim's neck and puncturing a main artery. Patterson and a few of his workers would follow the blood until they found the scattered bones and torn clothing.

"Sometimes, however, we would part the grasses and see a severed head," one worker remembered. "Nothing, not even one's most terrible nightmares, could match the horror of such a scene."

Not surprisingly, many of the workers fled in terror and returned to India. Although Patterson begged them to stay, they refused to continue working in a place they were certain was home to a pair of devils. Patterson knew he had no other choice but to hunt down and kill the Tsavo man-eaters, no matter how long it took—and it would take nearly nine months. After endless trips into the savannah to uncover the lions' hiding place, Patterson finally came across a grisly but welcome sight as he approached a small cave.

"Around the entrance and inside the cavern I was thunderstruck to find a number of human bones, with here and there a copper bangle such as the natives wear. Beyond all doubt, it was the man-eaters' den!"

Not long after this discovery, Patterson tracked the lions and shot them. From nose to tail tip, both cats were over nine feet long. Their huge paws were nearly three times as big as a human hand, with sharp three-inch claws. When Patterson looked into the mouths of the dead lions, he shuddered to see the long, sharp teeth that had killed so many men. One witness claimed to have seen bits of human hair and bone still stuck between the rows of teeth.

The story of the Tsavo man-killers had become so widespread and famous that everyone wanted to see these beasts. For days, Kenyan villagers lined up to see the devil cats. Eventually, both lions would be preserved through taxidermy and displayed in frighteningly lifelike hunting poses. You can still see them today in the Field Museum of Natural History in Chicago, Illinois.

The workers from India had good reason to fear the lions of Kenya. For thousands of years, Indians had lived in dread of a big cat of their own—the tiger. While it is just as rare for tigers to hunt humans for food as it is for lions, sometimes it happens. Barely eight years after the attacks of the Tsavo lions, a female tiger in India set out on a human-eating rampage that would place her in the *Guinness World Records.*

This big tigress had reportedly already eaten 200 victims in an area bordering India known as Nepal. When she was finally driven out of that region, she settled near Champawat, a town in India. There, she quickly and quietly proceeded to attack and eat another 236 victims. Unlike the Tsavo lions, whose roars could be heard nearly five miles away, this tiger moved soundlessly through the town's alleys and back roads. She gave no warning of her approach, and her method of killing was so quick that her victims rarely made a sound.

"We sat inside our hut one night because of the rains," one Champawat resident remembered. "My brother and I were talking quietly, smoking our pipes. When some ashes fell from my pipe onto the bed, I turned around to clean them off. When I turned back, my brother was gone! It had not been more than ten seconds, and he had not been more than ten feet away from me."

The tiger is the biggest of the big cats, often weighing up to 660 pounds, with four-inch sharp fangs. A single bite from a tiger has been known to crush the heavy backbone of a cow. It certainly did not take much effort for the Champawat tigress, as she would become known, to instantly kill her human targets. A quick, well-placed bite to the neck would not allow her victims even one second to cry out. To those who lived in Champawat, the tiger was like a mysterious, ghastly spirit that haunted the town night after night. People began staying up all night, banging drums and building roaring fires to keep the ghost tiger away. Still, in the morning light, another person would be missing.

Unlike the Tsavo lions, the Champawat tigress was not particularly difficult to track down. Tigers tend to eat their kills over the course of a few days, returning again and again to snack on the carcass, rather than, like lions, eating the kill all at once. A famous hunter of man-eating tigers, Jim Corbett, knew that if he could follow the trail of one of the tigress's kills, all he would have to do was wait for her to return. In the summer of 1907, Corbett was brought to India from England to do just that.

The Champawat tigress's final victim was a 16-year-old girl. Corbett walked into the jungle toward the place the tiger had been seen dragging the girl's body away. Near a puddle of blood, Corbett spotted the girl's necklace. Just past that, caught in some thorny bushes, were long strands of the girl's black hair. Corbett continued following these clues for several hundred yards. Then, rounding a corner, he came across a terrible sight. Surrounded by bits of bone and blood was the girl's left leg.

"In all the years I have hunted man-eaters," Corbett later wrote, "I have not seen anything as pitiful as that young leg bitten off a little below the knee as clean as though severed by the stroke of an axe."

Corbett was so disturbed that he didn't even notice the tigress standing on a ledge above him, barely 15 feet away. In her mouth was what was left of the girl. When Corbett heard the tigress growl, he lifted his gun to fire. But the tiger dashed away and then disappeared up a rocky mountainside to her hiding place.

The next morning, Corbett returned to the mountainside. With him were three hundred men with guns, tin cans, rocks, and whistles. For nearly an hour, the men made as much noise as they could while Corbett waited, his gun aimed. As Corbett anticipated, the tiger finally emerged from the rocky area where he had last seen her. Three gunshots later, the Champawat tigress was dead.

In the town and neighboring villages, people lined the streets as the carcass of the tiger was wheeled through on a cart. But there was no celebrating. Though the Indian people feared tigers, they also respected them. Now they felt no joy in seeing one killed. In fact, after the tiger was skinned, many people took bits of the tiger's bones to make into protective charms for their children.

Even Jim Corbett would eventually turn away from hunting and work, instead, to help protect the decreasing tiger population. Sometimes he regretted that his famed hunting had drawn so much attention to the very rare occurrences of big cats feeding on humans. During the following decades, many big game hunters would use the examples of the Tsavo lions and the Champawat tigress as excuses to kill thousands of these magnificent cats. In reality, tigers and lions typically have no interest in human flesh. If anything, they prefer to stay as far away from people as possible.

What, then, drove these cats to not only eat humans, but also to choose humans over other more natural prey? In the case of the tigress, the answer was obvious to Jim Corbett only moments after shooting her. As he looked into her mouth, he saw that both of her right canine teeth (the biggest and sharpest teeth) had been broken, most likely from an old gunshot wound. This had made it difficult, if not impossible, for the tiger to kill bigger, tougher game. Humans, however, were easier to kill, and their flesh was softer to chew.

As for the Tsavo lions, no one knows for certain why they turned into man-killers. One theory is that the two lions developed a taste for humans after finding the unburied bodies of Indian railroad workers. So many workers died of malaria that there was not always time for a proper burial. In fact, nearly two-thirds of these workers died while in Kenya. Often, bodies were buried hastily in shallow graves. These would have been easy for wild animals to dig up.

Still, a more common theory was, once again, that injuries from old gunshot wounds had made hunting normal prey difficult for the young lions. Examination of the lions showed an infected shoulder wound on one and broken teeth on the other. This was probably yet another case of big cats turning man-killers when they were faced with choosing either starving to death or settling for easier prey.

As big game hunting and safaris became increasingly popular in the twentieth century, there were more and more incidents of lions, tigers, and even leopards and cheetahs preying on humans after being injured by hunters. Some people, particularly natives, liked to believe that these attacks were a kind of revenge on humans. But it is doubtful that these cats had any sense of what revenge was—they were simply hungry.

"It is sad to realize," one observer later wrote, "that man's attempt to kill these big cats drove the cats, in turn, to kill man."

EIGHT LEGS
OF TERROR

Preview

Nothing says "terror"
like a big hairy spider the
size of a dinner plate . . .
unless it's a spider that has
gigantic sharp fangs and
can stand on its hind legs.
Or perhaps true terror is
defined by a tiny spider
whose venom can rot
human flesh, leaving
a gaping wound around
its bite. Meet your worst
spider nightmares in
this chapter.

EIGHT LEGS OF TERROR

Why do spiders freak out so many of us? It is estimated that nearly 30 percent of women and 20 percent of men are not just nervous about these eight-legged creatures—they're absolutely terrified of them. This irrational fear of spiders (known as "arachnophobia") can turn otherwise calm adults into screaming, frantic children. Just the sight of an old spider web is enough to make them refuse to enter a room. They approach innocent activities like hiking and camping with great anxiety. Cleaning out a garage or attic is absolutely out of the question.

"They move too fast for their size."

"There are just too many legs."

"They can run sideways, so you can never tell where they're headed."

"They drink the blood of their prey."

These are just some of the reasons people give for their fear of spiders. Of course, it doesn't help that many spiders do bite, and some are even poisonous. However, of the more than 50,000 *(50,000!)* types of spiders on earth, only a dozen are actually dangerous to humans. And even the bites of these dozen spiders rarely lead to anything more serious than discomfort or temporary illness. In fact, barely two people a year, worldwide, die from spider bites.

However, those who hate spiders will tell you it's not the poison they fear: it's something else. It's the creepiness, the mystery, and the hidden dark world of the spider that send a chill down the spine.

Which spiders are the very worst? Well, that depends on your definition of "worst." But surely one of the following four spiders will fit that dreaded definition.

It had been a long, hard week at work. After dinner and an hour of TV, Aaron, the parts manager at a Kansas auto repair shop, was ready for bed. The next day was Sunday, and he planned to sleep far past his usual 6 a.m. wakeup time. A bachelor, Aaron wasn't the world's greatest housekeeper. He'd washed his sheets recently but had left them lying in a tangled pile on the floor. Now he threw them carelessly on the bed and crawled in, intending not to move until at least noon.

It didn't work out that way. At about 3 a.m., Aaron jerked awake, startled by the sensation of something running up his thigh. Instinctively he slapped at his leg, only to feel a mild sting, like being poked with a tiny needle. He threw back the sheet and fumbled for the light, but the culprit had vanished. All he saw was a red bump on his thigh, much like a large mosquito bite.

Muttering in disgust, Aaron managed to get back to sleep, after thoroughly shaking out his bedding. But by 6 a.m., he was awake again. He felt a little queasy. The "mosquito bite" was now huge, about ten inches across. Aaron canceled his plans for the day and spent Sunday lying on the couch, channel-surfing and napping.

On Monday Aaron dragged himself to work. As he said later, "It was a bug bite, for Pete's sake. I couldn't believe it was really a big deal." By noon, he was in agony. He had a deep, stabbing pain in his thigh "as though someone were poking me with a knife." He limped into the restroom and took off his jeans to examine the bite.

What he saw horrified him. The entire top of his thigh was swollen, hot, and terrifically painful. At the center of the red area was a crater.

"The tiny bite mark had turned into a purple-black hole in my leg, a hole as big as my fist. It was covered with these really sick-looking blisters. All I could think was that it looked like the top of a volcano that had erupted."

A coworker rushed Aaron to the hospital. Doctors cut into the bite area and removed as much dead tissue as they could. But the next day Aaron was worse. He was taken to surgery again, where doctors were even more aggressive, cutting away dead flesh from an area the size of a 12-inch dinner plate.

"They had to stop the poison from spreading," Aaron explained. "That meant removing it from my body. Unfortunately, a good chunk of my leg went with it."

After the second surgery, Aaron's condition improved quickly. His temperature returned to normal, although he was weak and exhausted. Doctors began planning a series of skin grafts and plastic surgeries to cover the gaping wound in his thigh. The repairs would take a long time, but Aaron would live.

"I'll always have a heck of a scar on my thigh," he says today. "But if I hadn't gotten to the hospital when I did, I could have lost my entire leg, and maybe my life. All from a little bug bite!"

What had happened to Aaron? Because he didn't see (or, better yet, capture) the "bug" that bit him, it is impossible to be absolutely sure. But given his symptoms, Aaron was most likely the victim of a small but dangerous creature: the brown recluse spider. This tiny spider lives up to its name. A "recluse" is a person (or, in this case, a spider) that prefers to hide away from others and live alone. The brown recluse's favorite hiding places are in dark corners, in closets, and, as Aaron discovered, inside clothing or piles of laundry.

The spider's appearance is pretty unremarkable. It's small and dull brown, but it does have one slightly unusual feature. On its back, near its eyes, is a marking that looks something like a fiddle. For this reason, the brown recluse is sometimes called the "fiddleback" spider. But what really stands out about this bland-looking little spider is its bite.

"Imagine an acid that slowly dissolves skin and fat and muscle, finally leaving a big raw hole," said a doctor. "That's the result of an untreated recluse bite. It's the worst for small children. Some have completely lost noses and ears."

The good news is that there is anti-venom as well as treatment for this spider's scary bite. Most patients end up with little more than a small scar and a frightening memory. If left completely untreated, the bite may cause death in children, but there has never been a proven case of death by brown recluse. There have been a few cases where young children have died from badly infected spider bites. However, there was never any proof that the bite was, in fact, from a recluse.

And the bad news? A brown recluse may be your neighbor. These spiders live only in the United States. Their range is mostly throughout the Midwest and then south all the way to the Gulf of Mexico. If you're in one of the states where the brown recluse lives, there are two things to remember. First, if you discover a strange and painful bug bite on your body, see a doctor. And, second, don't leave your clothes and bed sheets in a pile on the floor—a recluse could move in!

In the rainforests of South America, explorers in the 1800s came upon a horrible sight. It was something straight out of their most terrifying nightmares. They had heard a high-pitched bird call. It sounded as though the bird was struggling. Then there was complete silence. As the explorers rounded a corner near where the call had come from, they jumped back a foot or two and gasped.

Just in front of a small rock burrow, the biggest spider they had ever seen was calmly eating a small bird. Four of the spider's long legs held the lifeless bird in place while the spider's long fangs sank into the bird's neck. The brown body of the spider was covered in spiky fur, and from leg to leg, it was nearly as big as a dinner plate. As the explorers gawked at this monster spider in horror, it let out an angry hiss and scurried back into its burrow, hauling the bird with it.

Based on this first sighting, explorers named this spider the goliath bird-eating spider. And it certainly is a giant. A member of the tarantula family, it holds the honor of being the biggest spider on earth. However, unlike most spiders, it doesn't weave a web to catch its prey. Instead, goliaths weave a thin mat and place it a foot or so from their burrows. Then they attach a single silky thread to the mat. After attaching the other end of the thread to one leg, the goliaths retreat to their little caves to relax. As soon as a small animal (bird, mouse, lizard) steps on the mat, a vibration is sent along the thread. This alerts the goliath, and it quietly springs up and begins to hunt.

The goliath bird-eating spider hunts very much like a lion. It carefully stalks and prowls. It slinks along close to the ground and freezes when the prey turns its way. Finally, it pounces, wraps its long legs around the prize, and delivers several deep bites. At this point, the goliath becomes all spider. It injects its venom into the prey, turning all of its victim's organs into a soupy liquid. Then the huge spider sucks down the goo, leaving nothing but a little pile of bones and skin and feathers.

As ghastly as this all sounds, the goliath is really pretty harmless to humans. The little brown hairs on its body are actually more dangerous than its bite. When it is frightened, the goliath will shoot these hairs at an enemy. If, by chance, these lodge in the human eye, they can cause a lot of problems. But the bite of a goliath? It causes less pain than a mild bee sting. And more often than not, a goliath is shy and gentle around humans. For this reason, some people think the goliath bird-eating spider makes a nice pet.

Not really thinking that a huge bird-eating tarantula sounds like your idea of a cuddly pet? Then how about having one for dinner? In some parts of the world where big spiders are common, a plate of deep-fried tarantulas is considered a real treat. Diners are instructed to eat the long crunchy legs first, one by one. Then it's time to take a big bite of spider body. It may be a little gooey at first, but some salt and garlic should make it a bit tastier.

Yum! Eat up!

Eating spiders or keeping them as fuzzy pets may be popular in some parts of the world, but not in Australia. The Land Down Under is home to the deadliest spiders on earth, and they certainly never show up on a dinner plate unless they've crawled there unexpectedly.

Most dreaded is the Sydney funnel-web spider. This is a hairy, thick black spider with oversized sharp fangs. The fangs are curved so that when the funnel-web takes a bite, it hangs on. The more its prey struggles to escape, the deeper the fangs and the venom sink into the victim. And the venom of this Australian spider is deadly. It is one of the very few spiders on earth whose poison can kill a human. Once the venom gets into the bloodstream, it can cause death by heart failure in less than a few hours.

Making this spider even more frightening is its aggressive, even bullying, behavior. When threatened or merely approached, it rears up on its hind legs and waves its long front legs in the air. Then it pulls its body back to show off its impressive fangs. Surrounding these knife-sharp fangs is a circle of blood-red hair. Top off this frightening display with the fact that the funnel-web spider often enjoys hanging out in the garages, backyards, and basements of Sydney residents. And from time to time, the funnel-web spider likes to nap in shoes or shirtsleeves. Not surprisingly, this is one much-dreaded spider.

To be fair, though, the streets of Sydney are not really crawling with these feared creatures. In fact, female funnel-web spiders rarely even leave their webs. Like the goliath bird-eating spider, they dangle a thin thread to alert them when prey is outside their web. However, they are fast and deadly enough to catch their dinner (bugs, other spiders, small lizards) right at their own doorstep. The female then retreats into her funnel-shaped web, where she will wait for a male funnel-web spider to find her.

It is the wandering search of the male funnel-web spider that brings it into contact with people. And, as bad luck would have it, the male is about six times more poisonous than the female. The warmer and wetter the weather, the more active these male spiders become. In January (summertime in Australia) 2010, unusually warm and rainy conditions brought what was known as "the invasion of the funnel-webs" right into downtown Sydney. Before long, the spiders began showing up in homes and yards.

"It was worse than my worst nightmare," recalled a young woman named Carolyn.

Carolyn was working in her small garden behind her house one afternoon. The wind had scattered leaves throughout her flowerbeds, so she was picking the leaves out in handfuls. Because she was afraid of spiders in general and well aware of the specific danger of the funnel-webs, Carolyn wore rubber gloves as she worked.

"What I didn't know was just how strong and sharp those fangs are!" Carolyn would later say.

As she lifted another pile of leaves and tossed them into a trashcan, she felt a very slight prick on the end of her thumb. There, hanging from Carolyn's glove and still in its attack posture, was a male funnel-web spider. It had bitten right through her heavy glove.

"It's an understatement to say I was panicked," Carolyn remembered. "I had heard that a bite could lead to death in twenty minutes. Of course, now I know that that is just one of those spider myths that get passed around. But I didn't know it at the time."

Because Carolyn lived only two blocks from a major hospital, she decided she would run to the emergency room. Certainly, she thought, she could get there within twenty minutes. It would be faster than waiting for an ambulance, and she didn't own a car. What happened next would definitely motivate Carolyn to virtually sprint to the hospital.

"I had shaken the spider off by that point, so I pulled off the gloves and threw them on the ground," Carolyn said. "Then I grabbed my rain jacket off the patio table. I rushed through the house, grabbed my purse, and took off. As I ran down the street, I put the jacket on. I don't even know why. I guess it was just a habit. And then . . . I could not believe it."

Carolyn felt a sharp sting on her forearm. At first, she thought she was just jumpy and imagining things. She instinctively slapped at the sting. Then she could feel something running down her arm.

"I'm quite certain that I must have looked like a madwoman. Out crawled another funnel-web spider from my sleeve. It must have crept inside my jacket while I was working. So now I was flailing my arms, running down the street, and probably screaming. I barely remember making it to the hospital. I was so sure that I was going to die."

Luckily for Carolyn, Sydney has the largest supply of funnel-web spider anti-venom in

Australia. In fact, hospitals are so well equipped, and medical staffs are so well educated about these spider bites, that no one has died from a funnel-web bite in decades. Carolyn would feel sick for a while, and the two bites would be painful and puffy, but within a week, her life was back to normal—well, almost normal.

"I can't say that the experience made me any more afraid of spiders than I had already been," Carolyn admitted. "But it definitely made me a little more afraid of gardening!"

When we think of dangerous spiders, the classic scary spider that most often comes to mind is the black widow. As opposed to the funnel-web spiders, it is the female black widow, not the male, that carries the dangerous venom. Males carry very little venom, and what they do possess is quite weak. However, it has been estimated that the female black widow's poison is fifteen times stronger than that of a rattlesnake!

For this reason, most people assume that black widows are killers. The truth is that it is extremely rare for anyone to actually die from a widow bite. Usually, there is just some pain around the bite. If the bite is untreated, there may be a few days of sickness. After all, a black widow is barely the size of a fingertip. And her fangs are so small that those who are bitten by her often don't even realize it. True, the widow's venom may be potent, but she really can't inject much of it into a human.

The black widow becomes a bit more gruesome, however, when she deals with her prey. To the human eye, the black widow's web looks like a big mess. It is not one of those beautiful lacy webs other spiders weave. It looks more like the broken remains of an old cobweb. But it is actually a very carefully constructed and intricate series of traps. Every silken strand the black widow weaves has a specific purpose. And there are literally thousands of strands that make up her web. Scientists have studied the black widow's astounding web design for years and still can't quite figure it out. That's pretty amazing for a spider with a brain the size of a pinhead.

Black widows particularly enjoy building their traps over anything that has a bad smell and might attract the flies, crickets, and other bugs it eats. Above trash containers, near dumps, and around rotting wood are choice spots. Another irresistible location is across the toilet seat of an outhouse. As one can imagine, this has led to more than a few black widow bites on the rear ends of surprised campers, hunters, and hikers.

The widow waits just outside of her trap-filled web. Unlike most spiders that have four to six eyes, the widow has only two very weak eyes. She is nearly blind. But as insects and other prey fall into her trap, the widow senses the smallest vibrations on each thread. Instantly, she knows the size, location, and strength of her prey. Each strand of the web is covered with sticky glue that snares and then entangles struggling insects. The widow crawls close, sizes up her catch, and throws out several more threads. These act as ropes to tie down her prey. Then the black widow sinks her tiny fangs into the body of her victim and unleashes her awesome poison.

The unbelievable strength of a black widow's web, combined with her venom, makes her able to bring down prey as much as 50 times her own size. This small spider has been observed feasting on everything from huge moths to adult mice. Still, her most famous victim is only a quarter her size. In addition, hoping she will notice, it walks willingly into her web. It is the male black widow.

"Honestly, the black widow does not eat her mate that often," explained one spider expert. "But it just seems so cruel when she does. So that is what we remember, and that is how she got her name."

The fate of the male black widow depends mostly on whether the female is hungry after mating. If she has recently eaten, the male wanders back out of her web, unharmed. But if she is ready for a meal, her mate is no different from any other creature she finds in her web. And if she is particularly hungry, she may even begin killing the poor male right in the middle of mating.

Still, in spite of her cruel and ravenous ways, the black widow, like all spiders, serves a very important purpose. She helps control the population of destructive insects such as ants, grasshoppers, and beetles. And she even does her part, in a big way, to cut down on poisonous spiders.

"After mating, the black widow will lay an egg sac full of maybe 1,000 eggs," said the spider expert. "Remember—this could be in your garage or backyard. And she lays eight to ten egg sacs every year. That's a lot of black widows!"

Like any good mother, the black widow guards the eggs closely for two to four weeks. She fiercely threatens anyone or anything that gets too close to her 1,000 eggs. Then, in keeping with her reputation, the black widow calmly observes the eggs hatching and the tiny spiders emerging . . . and she eats about 990 of them.

BIG PAIN IN
TINY PACKAGES

Preview

Deep in the jungles of South
America live the biggest
ants on earth. Their sting is
said to create the worst pain
known to humans. Yet every
year, an ancient tribe gathers
these ants by the hundreds.
On the other side of the
world, one or two stings of
the Japanese giant hornet can
send a person to the hospital.
And yet people regularly
invade the hornets' nests.
Why would anyone want
to bother these insects—
risking pain and even death?

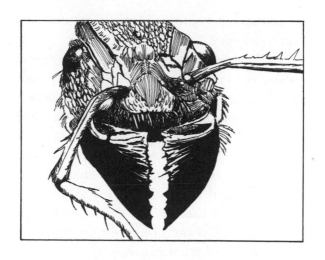

BIG PAIN IN TINY PACKAGES

Our planet is absolutely crawling with bugs. At any given moment, there are about 10,000,000,000,000,000,000 (that's ten *quintillion*) insects digging, scurrying, and flying around the earth. If that's too big a number to imagine, here are some facts to make it clearer. For every human being alive right now, there are 200 million insects. For every pound of humans on earth, there are 300 pounds of bugs. A single termite nest in South America can hold more termites than there are people in New York City. And the common housefly can hatch more than 500 eggs—*every day*!

Luckily, there are two very good things about insects. First, of the eight million kinds of bugs that exist, very few are dangerous to humans. Second, insects are incredibly important. They crawl through soil, making it ready to grow plants. They carry pollen from plant to plant, creating new growth all over the earth. What's more, the good insects keep the bad insects in check by eating them by the billions every hour of every day. Without insects, life on our planet would come to a screeching halt.

Even so, people are bugged by bugs. At best, insects can be annoying. No one likes gnats zooming around his or her head. And seeing a cockroach in the kitchen is pretty gross. At worst, however, insects can be deadly. While it's true that only a fraction of the bugs on our planet are dangerous, that fraction packs quite a punch. The mosquito is a fairly harmless nuisance in the United States. But in other parts of the world, particularly Africa, it is a major killer. Because it draws blood out of humans, the mosquito also spreads disease. The most dangerous disease it spreads is malaria. Close to two million people die from malaria every single year. This makes the tiny mosquito tremendously dangerous.

Sharks and crocodiles are nothing compared to this little bug.

Somewhere between the annoying insects and the disease-spreading insects are the ones that probably scare us the most—the stinging and biting insects. Diving hornets with huge stingers and angry swarms of yellow jackets are the stuff of nightmares. It is extremely rare for people to be killed by stinging bugs unless they are allergic to the venom of a particular bug. Still, gruesome stories abound.

There was the 66-year-old man who ran over a yellow jacket nest while he was mowing. He was found dead four hours later. Thousands of furious yellow jackets still covered his body and the mower. And there is the handful of tales about wasps that chase their victims for up to a mile while covering them with stings until they drop. Now and then a bizarre killer-bug story pops up. Several years ago, a farm worker in Bolivia fell asleep beneath a tree after he had had too much to drink. Unfortunately, he had lain down right on top of a huge anthill that housed thousands of very aggressive biting ants. About 20,000 stings later, the dead worker was discovered.

Still, 99 percent of the time, run-ins with stinging insects are much less dramatic. The victim suffers a frantic moment of fear and a bit of pain. However, on occasion, some unfortunate victims get in the way of some truly hideous bugs. And some of these little monsters can deliver a ton of pain.

Imagine, for example, an ant with a pair of enormous pincers on its head. The pincers look like a vise. On the rear of this ant is a sharp pointed barb—its stinger. Combine this with a very long body that looks like a wingless wasp, and you have the dreaded bullet ant. Bullet ants are the biggest ants on earth, with the biggest stingers. They live in parts of South America, and their bite is legendary. They hold the honor of having the most painful sting of any insect alive.

"I've never been shot," claimed one victim, "but it couldn't be any worse than the bullet ant's bite. After all, that's how it got its name. They say it feels just like a bullet slamming into you."

While this ant was named for the pain it inflicts, it has another nickname: the "24-hour" ant. Searing, burning pain from a sting can last up to a full day. During this time of misery, victims may shake, sweat, and throw up. And as if this isn't enough horror, the bullet ant shrieks right before it stings. Yes, that's right—a shrieking ant. It's the last thing you'll hear before a day of intense pain.

So this definitely sounds like an insect that any sane person would avoid at all costs, right?

Not really.

Deep in the jungles of Brazil is an ancient tribe that goes in search of these hideous ants quite often. For a teenage boy in this tribe, the only way he can officially enter manhood is by enduring the pain of the bullet ant without screaming. Not just the pain of one sting . . . or even 20. Boys must willingly allow dozens of bullet ants to sting them repeatedly! This ceremony of passage to adulthood is a time of both celebration and terror. And it has been taking place for hundreds of years.

The adult men of the tribe go into the jungle the day before the ceremony. Clustered around the trunks of trees are the mounded anthills of the bullet ant. Carefully, the men dip sticks into a hill and pull out dozens of angry ants. Then the ants are placed in large buckets containing a mixture that puts them to sleep. That night, the tribal leaders take these sleeping ants one by one and sew them into large gloves. The stingers face inward into and through the gloves, while the ants' heads face outward. Twenty to thirty bullet ants are sewn into each glove. By morning light, the ants have awakened and are struggling furiously. The ritual of pain now begins.

Boys, most of them 15 to 17 years old, are painted with exotic and frightening designs. Scorpions, huge ants, and snakes cover their chests and backs. Stripes, like bright red tears, drip down their faces. The tribal people gather around. They chant, sing, and shout. Some of the older men give final quiet words of advice to the frightened boys. Then it is time.

Each boy walks forward, his hands in front of him. Quickly, the ant-filled gloves are slipped onto both hands. Now the boys must endure ten minutes of non-stop stinging. If they cry out or throw off the gloves, they fail this test of manhood. Some of the boys hide their eyes behind strips of white cloth so that no one will see their tears. Others simply bow their heads and shake. However, the many stings of the bullet ant are only the beginning. And they are mild in comparison to what the boys will endure over the next 24 hours.

In 2008, a British adventurer named Steve Brackshall decided to head down to Brazil to take part in one of these rituals. During his past adventures, Steve had been charged by elephants, bitten by poisonous snakes, and chased by sharks. But nothing compared to his fear of the bullet ant ritual—or the pain it created.

"I had suffered several hundred stings, and all

of a sudden I went beyond pain," Steve recalled. "I can't describe it using simple words. All I can do is describe what happened."

Steve was twice the age and twice the size of the boys around him. As he looked at them through his blurring vision, he was stunned at how calm they were compared to him. Within a few minutes of being stung, Steve fell apart.

"First, I started wailing; then, once that had passed, the floodgates opened. I was sobbing, shaking uncontrollably, and convulsing. You could see the poison kicking in. My muscles started quivering, my eyelids drooped, and my lips went numb. I started to drool, and suddenly I wasn't responding to anything at all. My legs wouldn't hold me up. If there'd been a machete nearby, I'd have chopped off my arms to escape the pain."

Still, 24 hours later, Steve and all the boys were all right. Their hands were swollen and red, but the pain was nearly gone. No sickness or damage remained. For a sting that is so overwhelming, the speedy recovery is amazing. Most insects with powerful stings leave a painful or itchy reminder for weeks.

One scientist explained the bullet ant's unusual sting: "Most stinging spiders and insects use their poison to paralyze prey. But the bullet ant uses its poison only for defense. So, over millions of years, its poison has been perfected into something pretty unique. It creates a terrible growing pain that makes the interfering animal think it's been horribly wounded. As a result, the animal backs off immediately. A day later, everything is fine. The poison hurts badly for a while, but it's not that strong. No one's ever been killed or even gotten really sick from bullet ant stings."

But for those visiting the Amazon and the jungles of Brazil, the bullet ant remains something best seen from a distance—or not seen at all.

"All I can say is, thank God those things don't fly!" claimed one visitor after safely viewing an anthill through her binoculars.

And speaking of horrible flying insects, how about a huge hornet with venom powerful enough to melt human flesh? This is the Japanese giant hornet. It can grow up to two inches long, with a three-inch wingspan—as wide as a hand. Its stinger is thick, sharp, and nearly half an inch long. Those who have been stung by this insect have compared the experience to a red-hot nail being slammed into their skin.

These monster-sized hornets have been called the most aggressive and dangerous flying insects on earth. When threatened by a human, they have been known to locate a person's eyes and spray their venom directly into them. Once the victim is temporarily blinded and unable to run away, the giant hornet attacks—more than once. Unlike some other stinging insects, this hornet does not die after stinging. It is able to inflict pain again and again.

But what if the hornet doesn't get to your eyes? Think you might be able to run away from it? Think again. In addition to being the biggest and fiercest hornet on earth, it is also the fastest. If it's irritated enough, it will zoom after its victim at speeds of more than 25 miles per hour. And these aren't just quick bursts of angry speed that fade away. Japanese hornets have been known to fly up to 60 miles a day in search of food or shelter. In rare cases, they will spend hours chasing an intruder. And though the hornets will not enter water to follow their victim, they have been seen hovering patiently above a lake or river. Their brains may be tiny, but hornets know that their victim will surface eventually.

Still, how dangerous can one of these scary hornets be? Quite dangerous, actually. Just a few stings can release enough poison to land a person in the hospital. If not treated quickly enough, this hornet's venom can work like an acid. It can eat away skin and even dissolve bone. And, unfortunately, angering one Japanese hornet does not mean being chased by only one Japanese hornet. When this insect is upset, it releases an unusual chemical into the air. Acting like an alarm, the chemical drifts back to the hornet's nest, home to 500 to 700 more hornets. Suddenly, one irritated hornet is transformed into a killer swarm.

In Japan and parts of China, the only places this insect lives, around 40 people a year die from these hornets' stings. Most who die have a severe allergy to bee and wasp (hornets are wasps) venom. They may have been stung only once and simply couldn't get to a hospital in time. However, every year, there are also people who die terribly gruesome deaths after being chased and attacked by determined swarms. These poor victims are literally stung to death.

To be fair to Japanese hornets, they do not attack humans unless seriously provoked or accidentally cornered. Fans of this wasp (yes, there really are some) point out that this insect is usually reluctant to use its stinger. In fact, the Japanese giant hornet can be picked up and handled gently. It may even walk across one's arm slowly, sensing and smelling curiously before flying away.

What, then, transforms these normally calm insects into enraged killers? And who on earth would provoke them on purpose?

"Egg collectors," explained a Japanese author. "In some parts of Japan, it is considered quite a delicacy to eat the larvae (which hatch from the eggs) of the giant hornet. And like any creature on our planet, these hornets will kill to protect their young."

In addition, it's not just the eggs that bring a high price. Recently, a sports drink that uses the fluids in a Japanese hornet's stomach has become popular in Japan.

"Athletes swear that it gives them more endurance and helps them run very fast," claimed the author. "If I were the one capturing these hornets, I'd definitely be drinking plenty of it!"

All joking aside, no one has ever outrun a giant hornet swarm attack. Although the egg and hornet collectors take many precautions, there are deaths every year. Not long ago, a collector's body was found about a quarter mile from a hornet nest. He had been stung more than 1,400 times. His body was so swollen that his clothing was torn at the seams. And his eyes and tongue had partially melted because of the huge amounts of hornet venom pumped into him.

But it could be worse—if you were a bee.

Honeybees are the Japanese hornet's favorite food. Hornet attacks on bees are so vicious that they inspired a 2002 *National Geographic* special titled "Hornets from Hell." First, the giant insects surround a honeybee hive and confuse the tiny bees. Like noisy helicopters, the hornets hover, threatening, as the bees panic. Then the attack begins. Using its big, sharp jaws, a hornet snaps a bee's head and legs off and eats the body. One hornet can eat 40 honeybees in *one minute*. And a swarm of hornets can reduce a busy hive of 30,000 bees to a graveyard of heads and legs in less than an hour.

For many thousands of years, the Japanese hornet has lived mainly up in the mountains and in the deep forests of China and Japan. But as more and more land is developed for homes and businesses, the hornet's natural habitat is disappearing. As a result, the hornets have begun moving into the cities. They feast on garbage and build their homes in backyards and even on porches. They sting intruders, and they have killed several curious children who have poked sticks at their nests.

"No one likes to hear it, but it's a fact," said one scientist who studies insects. "Nature doesn't follow our rules. And when we interfere with its rules, we pay the price."

SNAPPING JAWS AND GLOWING EYES

Preview

Most of the dangerous animals on earth really have no interest in eating humans. They attack only because of fear or the desire to protect their young. However, there is one gruesome and terrifying exception. This creature tracks humans, lurks in dark water waiting for them, and kills them brutally. Meet the crocodile.

SNAPPING JAWS
AND GLOWING EYES

Two hundred million years ago, a terrifying reptile roamed parts of the earth. This car-sized monster was covered in rock-hard armor that could resist the claws and fangs of its enemies. But as tough as this skin was, it also contained a great many little soft sensors. These sensors could warn this creature of danger that may have been hundreds of yards away. Even more sensitive, the long nose of this animal could smell and track blood for miles.

This beast weighed nearly 2,000 pounds, and it could live for more than 100 years. Even though its walnut-sized brain and beady eyes never grew any bigger than they were at birth, the body of the creature *never* stopped growing! Reaching lengths of up to twenty feet, it lived on both land and water. And even though it was big, this monster could suddenly rocket toward its prey in lightning-fast bursts of speed.

And once this creature set its sights on its prey, the unfortunate dinner-to-be had very little chance of escape. This reptile had a mouth that could open wide enough to snap a deer or goat in half. In addition, inside its mouth were sharp fangs and sawing teeth. The force of this prehistoric monster's bite was nearly 500 pounds per square inch—ten times more powerful than a shark's bite. The only thing tougher than its bite was its ability to keep its jaws clamped around its prey. No matter how hard victims fought, they could not escape this creature's steel jaws.

Rounding out the horror of the beast were the murky and sometimes filthy waters that it called home. It often lurked in dark lakes and rivers, waiting for an unsuspecting animal to wander too close to the water's edge. Then, after the attack, this reptile was fond of hiding its kill in the tangled roots and rocks near the water's edge. It preferred the corpses of its prey to rot so that they would be easier to eat. And it was never difficult for this creature to see underwater or in the dead of night—it had special eyes that glowed red and saw through darkness.

As dinosaurs began to die out and finally fade into extinction, this reptile, for some reason, continued to thrive. No one can really explain why, but it may have had something to do with the fact that it was not exactly a picky eater. It hunted birds, fish, wild dogs, deer, snakes, and even other reptiles. It also had an amazing ability to digest nearly everything it swallowed, from feathers to hoofs to bones and even small stones. When early humans appeared, they too became an item on this fierce reptile's menu. Ancient fossils have revealed human bones inside this creature's stomach.

Millions of years passed. The earth changed; humans changed; nearly all the animals on the face of the earth changed dramatically—but not this one. It still lurks in dark waters. With its armor-plated skin and glowing eyes, it looks much the same as it did 200 million years ago. Today we know it as the crocodile, a true leftover from the age of dinosaurs.

This giant reptile has long haunted the nightmares of those people who share its habitat. Crocs make their homes in warm, tropical areas: along the River Nile in Africa, in some parts of

South America, in Australia, and even in the United States. The American crocodile (found in Florida), however, is not nearly as big or dangerous as the crocs found in other parts of the world.

Most animals that attack humans have no interest in eating them. These animals are usually defending territory, protecting young, or reacting out of fear. Other animals, such as bears and sharks, may take bites out of the people they attack, but typically they do not seek out humans as a source of food. Human flesh is really not a regular or desirable menu item for the great majority of animals.

Crocodiles are the exception. No other animal on the planet intentionally stalks and kills as many humans for food as the crocodile does.

The view from beneath murky water may not be the best, but a crocodile can smell and sense a warm-blooded creature from across a river. As long as a hungry crocodile senses that it can handle the size of the prey, it will attack anything that moves. And a crocodile can handle some sizeable prey. Once, hunters watched a large Nile croc leap out of the water and clamp onto the snout of a rhinoceros that was drinking at the water's edge. Usually, rhinos and crocs leave one another alone, but not on this particular afternoon.

"That rhino surely must have outweighed the croc by 2,000 pounds," one of the hunters commented, "but that didn't matter to the crocodile. It just held on, playing tug of war for nearly an hour."

As the rhinoceros grew tired, it began sliding, inch by inch, toward the water. Because crocodiles are built low to the ground, they can dig into the river mud with their strong hind legs and claws and maneuver thousands of pounds. Now the croc pulled the rhino's nose and mouth into the water, eventually drowning it without too much trouble.

"It was far too big for that one croc to eat the entire thing," the hunter said. "Still, the crocodile and several of his friends managed to tear some pretty good chunks off the drowned rhino. I suppose the rest was stowed somewhere to rot."

Although crocodiles can deliver a mighty bite, they can't chew. As a result, they will swallow whole anything they can.

"The inside of a croc's stomach is sort of a junkyard," one crocodile hunter wrote. "I have found everything from human jewelry to whole wart hogs to Coke bottles and three-pound rocks inside of them. One ten-footer even had a four-foot crocodile inside of him."

Clearly, then, humans are a relatively quick and easy-to-catch meal for crocs. However, in Australia, home to some of the largest and fiercest crocs on earth, and the United States, very few people are ever attacked by crocodiles. This is because people generally do not live or work within striking distance of crocs. And when people *are* near crocodile-infested waters, they usually take many precautions.

This is not the case in many parts of Africa. Villages are often situated close to the Nile or other bodies of water where crocodiles thrive. The people in these villages use this water daily for drinking, bathing, cleaning, and fishing. It is not unusual for crocodiles to lurk in the rivers and lakes, with only their eyes and the tips of their snouts above water. They remain motionless, waiting and watching and studying the villagers' patterns and habits. From the riverbanks, it is almost impossible to pick out a croc in dark waters. It looks exactly like an old log or a rock—until it suddenly charges out of the darkness and clamps down on its victim.

It is estimated that nearly one thousand Africans are eaten by crocodiles *every year!* It's hard to know exact numbers since the villagers rarely report attacks to authorities. In fact, death by crocodile is often shrugged off by many rural

Africans as simply an expected risk. They look at it much the same way we might casually consider the risk of a car accident on our way to work.

"I can't understand it," one American visitor to an Ethiopian village said. "It totally baffles me."

What this visitor was referring to was an incident that had happened only a week before he had arrived. A young Ethiopian woman and her sister had gone down to the river's edge near dusk to bathe and fill some jugs with water for use the next day. It was the same pattern they had followed every day for years—same place, same time. But this evening would not have the same ending.

The older sister threw a handful of pebbles into the blackish water. If a crocodile was prowling, this should startle it and scare it away. They had chased off a croc with rocks only a month earlier, so they believed this method was foolproof. But the sisters didn't see the 13-foot female crocodile lurking underwater. The croc had been carefully observing the riverbank and its activity for three days. She knew the sisters were coming. She had smelled them before she had seen them. And now, as the younger sister stepped knee-deep into the river, the big croc began creeping toward her.

There was no quiet splash, not even a ripple

of water to give the huge crocodile away. Able to hold their breath underwater for more than an hour, crocs take their time inching toward their prey. Now this one was within 20 feet of its victim, who laughed and chatted with her sister. Now ten feet away, the crocodile lifted only her eyes above the water's surface to estimate how far to leap and how quickly to open her jaws.

Then the river seemed to explode. The crocodile flung itself on the younger sister, grabbing her by the neck and dragging her beneath the surface of the water in less than two seconds. There was no time for the victim to scream or struggle. All the older sister could see in the dimming light was a trail of blood and then, further down the river, the huge crocodile surfacing with the limp form of her sister in its mouth.

"And yet," the American visitor reported, "the older sister returned the very next week to the very same spot to bathe and get water. When I asked her how she could possibly do that, she looked at me in surprise and said, 'That is what we do.'"

It is not unheard of for the same crocodile to return again and again to the same stretch of river in search of human victims. A crocodile hunter who was called in to hunt down a croc who had supposedly eaten hundreds of victims finally killed a monstrous 18-footer that had been lurking near the attack sites. Not sure whether he had the right croc, the hunter cut it open to inspect the contents of its stomach.

"Eleven brass arm rings, three wire armlets, an assortment of anklets, one necklace, fourteen human arm and leg bones, and three human spinal columns," the hunter wrote, were among the items still digesting in the croc's stomach. It certainly looked as though he had found the guilty crocodile.

But African natives who use the river for their livelihood are not the only ones who get attacked. There are many stories about those who meet their untimely deaths in the jaws of crocs. Tourists, careless fishermen and hunters, and unwary visitors have all been victims of hungry crocodiles.

In 1986, two British hunters set out after a 17-foot croc that had developed quite a nasty reputation. Villagers in Tanzania were convinced that this beast was more than just another dangerous man-eating crocodile. They believed it was truly evil, something sent directly from the devil himself. Spears, knives, and even bullets from a previous hunter's rifle had not been able to bring this monster down. It was impossible for the natives to understand. Why wouldn't this croc die?

"Most crocodiles' ability to hang on to the very last shreds of life would make a vampire jealous," an experienced crocodile hunter had written in 1978.

But, like the villagers, the two British hunters were not aware of this frightening characteristic of crocs. After tracking the crocodile down and shooting him twice in the head, the two hunters assumed he was dead. After all, one of the shots had blown off part of the croc's skull. Now the crocodile appeared to be stretched out lifeless on the riverbank. The two men slapped one another on the back, congratulating themselves, and prepared to take some photos.

Then, just as one of the men crouched down next to the croc to pose for a picture, the beast's powerful tail came to life. It swung wildly and knocked the hunter to the ground. Before the hunter had even one second to move away, the crocodile closed its jaws around his leg and scurried back into the river.

"I was too stunned to move at first," the victim's friend recalled. "And by the time I did, the croc had dragged him underwater. He surfaced just once, screaming, 'Shoot him! Shoot him!' Then I saw the croc open its mouth very wide and grab him around the neck. And that was it."

The doomed hunter was never seen again.

Twenty years earlier, a group of young and enthusiastic American Peace Corps volunteers were on a mission in Ethiopia. They had spent a long, hot day working in a local village. As the muggy evening began, a cool swim in the nearby Baro River was irresistible.

"They had been told again and again that the river was dangerous," one of the group's leaders remembered. "A woman had been killed only a few weeks earlier by a crocodile that was often seen on a nearby bank."

But the temptation of cool water was too much. And as far as anyone in the group could see, there was no crocodile on the bank. Surely if everyone stayed together and made a lot of noise and splashing, there would be no threat. However, one young man named Bill Olson decided to venture over to a small sandbar alone. He wanted to stand waist-deep and let the current run against him as he took in the awesome scenery.

The last person to see Olson alive was a hunter named Karl Luthy. Luthy noticed a man standing off by himself in the river. Luthy briefly wondered why anyone would take that kind of risk.

"When I looked back, maybe five minutes later, he was gone. There had never been a sound. He was just gone," Luthy said.

The Corps volunteers and Luthy began a frantic search for Olson, but no trace was found. Then, just before sunset, Luthy saw a large crocodile in the distance raise its massive head above the water. In its jaws was a lifeless carcass, but it was impossible to tell if it was human, much less the body of Bill Olson. Because of the growing darkness, Luthy decided to wait until the next day to hunt down the killer croc.

In the hot morning sun, the huge crocodile was sunning itself. Its stomach was clearly bloated from a recent meal. Luthy did not have much trouble killing it. Then came the gruesome task of cutting open the crocodile to inspect the contents of its stomach.

"There was no doubt, then, that this 13-foot crocodile was the one that had killed Olson," Luthy said, declining to comment on the exact details of what was found in the croc's belly. Olson's remains were then placed in a box and returned to the United States for burial.

"All I can say is that I'm glad I hadn't known this young man personally," Luthy concluded. "That would have been too hard to bear."

SOMETHING'S IN THE WATER

Preview

Going swimming? Watch where you step. Right under your foot, there could be a super-poisonous fish disguised as a stone.

And be careful where you swim—a monster jellyfish with invisible 60-foot tentacles may be waiting to sting you.

Thinking of dangling your hands in the water? Beware of the small razor-toothed fish that just might bite off a finger.

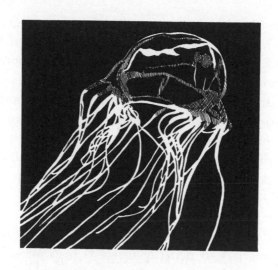

SOMETHING'S IN THE WATER

When it comes to scary animals in the water, the first things most of us think of are the big toothy creatures like sharks, orcas, and crocodiles. But sometimes pain and terror can come in much smaller packages. These tinier beasts don't have quite the star power that sharks and crocs command, but they can certainly do their share of damage.

Consider, for example, the stonefish.

Never heard of a stonefish? You're not alone. These slimy, ugly fish are not exactly popular in aquariums or fish stories. Imagine an old grey rock covered in dirt and moss. Now place that rock on the ocean floor and give it a huge mouth. Throw in some lumpy and warty skin, weird eyes, and a bunch of spines. Add some tremendously strong venom to the spines, and you've got a stonefish. Not only does the stonefish hold poison in the unlucky thirteen spines that stick out of its back; its entire body is covered with little bristles of poison. Even nicking a finger on the skin of a stonefish can lead to bad pain.

Stonefish are sneaky. They can camouflage themselves so perfectly that it is impossible to see them lying in wait for prey among the coral and rocks. They are able to turn the exact color of the coral or sand in which they are hiding. As hideously ugly as a stonefish is, it can become a lovely shade of pink or blue as it waits for dinner to swim by. However, once a stonefish spots its victim, it doesn't use its deadly spines to catch it. Instead, it remains hidden and motionless until a shrimp or a small fish swims within inches of its oversized mouth. Then, in a split second, the stonefish opens wide. It draws water into its cavernous mouth, creating tremendous suction. Shrimp and fish are literally vacuumed up whole.

Those dreaded spines of the stonefish are used only for defense. They lie flat along the fish until it senses a threat. Then the spines stand straight up. Merely brushing against these sharp barbs is enough to release venom strong enough to kill a person. In fact, the stonefish is believed to be one of the most poisonous fish in the sea. However, the pain that a stonefish can inflict is as frightening as its poison.

"I got spiked on the finger by a stonefish in Australia," one victim recalls. "A bee sting doesn't even compare. Imagine having each knuckle, then the wrist, elbow, and shoulder, being hit in turn with a sledgehammer over the course of about an hour. Then about an hour later, imagine taking a real kicking to both kidneys for about 45 minutes so that you couldn't stand or straighten up."

This was the reaction from what this victim called "the tiniest of nicks" by one of the stonefish's spines. Later, his hand would go numb, and it would stay that way for a week. Sharp pains in his kidneys would continue for years. Those who are unlucky enough to step directly on a stonefish and get the full force of its venom have described it as the worst pain known to humankind. It often begins as a sharp tingling that moves quickly up the leg. Within minutes, the pain feels like having thousands of needles jabbing into them all at once.

Just how bad *is* that kind of pain?

"We have seen patients that have begged to have their legs amputated," said a doctor in Australia, where stonefish are most common. "And they're not just saying that. They really mean it."

The good news is that modern medicine has developed both painkillers and anti-venom for the sting of a stonefish. Today, it is extremely unusual for anyone to die as a result of stepping on this ugly, hidden fish. However, if you are careless enough to wander barefoot in areas where stonefish lurk, you may find yourself thinking that death might be less painful!

What, then, could be worse than a stonefish? How about a four-eyed, nearly invisible sea creature with 60 ten-foot tentacles? This is the box jellyfish, also known as a sea wasp. As the sea wasp floats through murky seawater, its clear body and milky tentacles are almost impossible to spot. And it's really too bad that those tentacles are hard to see, because each one is covered with thousands of small cells. Each cell is packed with one of the most dangerous venoms known to exist.

Many scientists agree that the sea wasp is, in fact, the deadliest creature on earth. At any given time, a grown box jellyfish carries enough venom to kill 60 adult men. Its unique venom is made up of microscopic darts that can sink into whatever its tentacles touch. It's hard to believe that a creature that is nearly as delicate as a flower and 95 percent water can be so dangerous. But along the coast of Australia, these sea wasps gather in large numbers during the summer. And the foolish swimmer who ignores the warning signs posted on beaches may find his or her body wrapped in stinging tentacles.

Like the stonefish, the sea wasp stings humans only when they swim or wade directly into it. It is not an aggressive creature. It spends most of its time floating through the ocean in search of the small fish and shrimp it stings and eats. And it is not the brightest creature, either. In fact, a box jellyfish does not even have a brain. It relies completely on nerve cells to tell it when to release its poison darts. Obviously, it can't sting everything it touches, so its nerve cells react only to certain chemicals released by shrimp, fish, or human skin.

What's it like to be stung by this monster jellyfish?

"The pain is immediate," said one surfer who tangled with just a few of the thin tentacles of a young sea wasp. "It's a terrible prickling and burning pain that runs the length of wherever the tentacle has touched your skin. Think about having a blowtorch burning your skin for 20 minutes without stopping. That's the pain from just one or two small tentacles."

Quite often, the thin, fragile tentacles tear right off of the jellyfish and stick to the skin. But even when these tentacles are no longer attached to the living jellyfish, they are not dead. If they are not removed, they can continue releasing venom for up to an hour. Removing them is easy enough if you have the right tools. This is why gloves and bottles of vinegar can be found along some Australian beaches, next to signs warning of box jellyfish. Vinegar is the only known solution that will stop the stinging.

And in the days that follow, the stings swell and itch terribly. Victims may vomit, feel feverish, and have trouble breathing. Where the tentacles touched, flesh may burn away, leaving long raw streaks that can turn a bluish purple.

"I pretty much looked like I'd been whipped with a chain or something," claimed the surfer. "And I felt worse than that."

Of course, not everyone lives to describe the pain. The venom of the sea wasp is so fast-acting that some victims who are stung extensively never even make it back to shore. The poison rushes through the bloodstream far more quickly than that of even the most venomous snake on earth.

The venom attacks the heart and lungs, causing a nearly instant heart attack. It is not unusual for someone who really gets tangled in the tentacles of a box jellyfish to die within four minutes. And for those who don't die from heart failure, the pain is so intense that they often go into shock and drown before reaching the shore.

So what's the best protection from these killer jellyfish? Heavy-duty wetsuits or metallic diving gear? As it turns out, nothing quite that strong is needed. Since the box jellyfish ejects venom when it senses certain chemicals from our skin, all that's needed is something light to cover arms and legs and block the chemicals. Years ago, Australians discovered that nylon pantyhose work very well for this purpose. As a result, it's not at all uncommon to see lifeguards along the beaches in Australia wearing pantyhose with their swim trunks. Additionally, they cut off the toes of another pair and slip the pantyhose over their arms.

"Yeah, it was a little embarrassing at first," said one burly six-and-a-half-foot guard near Queensland, Australia. "But I'd rather be alive and embarrassed than dead and proud."

Not really that afraid of some ugly, spiny little fish or a fragile, brainless jellyfish? Then perhaps a six-foot super-poisonous sea snake would be more exciting. There are quite a few different snakes that live in the ocean, and all of them are poisonous. However, none quite compare to the beaked sea snake.

One of the more alarming characteristics of the beaked sea snake is that it's very difficult to tell its mouth from its tail. Because it can flatten and widen the end of its tail, there's no telling which end contains the fangs and the venom. And that's some wicked venom stored in this snake's jaws. Some scientists argue that the beaked sea snake's venom is the most poisonous snake venom on earth. It is nearly eight times stronger than the venom of a cobra. The tiniest drop can kill three people. And unlike the stonefish or the box jellyfish, a sea snake causes almost no pain when it bites. The poison starts to affect victims about forty minutes after they've been bitten. Suddenly everything looks blurry. The heart races wildly, and breathing slowly becomes impossible.

In spite of its venom, the beaked sea snake doesn't have particularly big fangs. However, it can open its mouth wide enough to take in fish nearly three times its own size. It chases after large fish, gives them a paralyzing bite, and then swallows them whole. Slow-moving catfish that crawl along the bottom of creeks and inlets near the ocean appear to be the beaked sea snake's favorite meal. And it is this snake's love of fish that usually brings into contact with humans.

"They used to call them 'net biters,'" said a fisherman who had seen more than his share of beaked sea snakes. "If you bring one up in a fishnet, they'll bite like crazy to break free. They'll chew holes in the nets, but that's better than bringing them on deck with the fish."

Often described as irritable and savage, an accidentally caught beaked sea snake has long been a terror to fishermen. It can move nearly as fast along the deck of a boat as it can in the water. And it is not shy about lunging and snapping at anyone who gets in its way. Fishermen attempting to throw the snake out of a net cannot tell which end is which. More than a few fishermen have been bitten when they have grabbed a sea snake's head instead of its tail. And here's something that makes this snake just a bit more terrifying: Even when its head is chopped off, it doesn't give up.

"You have never seen so many grown men scatter so fast," a South African fisherman said. "The snake was dumped out of a net, all six feet of him wriggling and angry. We'd seen them before, but not usually on the deck. That was just too close. So everyone backs up, and I take a big knife and chop that snake right in half. Everyone's cheering and relieved—until we suddenly see *both halves* moving. And there went the head, jaws wide open, right toward one of the men."

In fact, the beaked sea snake can still bite and deliver venom for up to an hour after being killed. The snake is no longer actually alive, but twitching nerves and muscles keep the snake moving and the jaws snapping.

"That is one cantankerous snake," the South African man concluded. "It's so fierce that it even refuses to die when its head is no longer attached to its body!"

Finally, there is the small freshwater terror, the piranha. This little razor-toothed fish has gotten more bad publicity than the stonefish, sea wasp, and beaked sea snake combined. In movies, it is presented as an ultra-vicious monster that can fly through the air and, in seconds, reduce humans to bare skeletons. Supposedly, it lurks in schools of thousands, just waiting for someone to dip his or her feet in the water so that it can gnaw all ten toes down to the bone.

As with most animals we fear, where the piranha is concerned, there is a whole lot of fiction mixed with fact.

It is true that, at times, the piranha can be terribly bloodthirsty and vicious. During periods of drought in South America, piranhas become very hungry. They will bite the fins off passing fish, snap chunks out of one another, and even eat their own young. And they have been observed gathering in schools of twenty or more (not thousands) and waiting for an unfortunate small animal to wander into the water for a drink. On rare occasions, very hungry piranhas will even latch onto the nose of a sick or injured cow and attempt to drag it into a river or lake.

What happens next is what makes the piranha so gruesome and so fascinating (in a horrible way) to us. Most predators kill their prey with a bite, a sting, or a fierce shake before beginning to eat, but the piranha eats its prey alive. Witnesses have described churning water turning red with blood when schools of these sharp-toothed fish go into a feeding frenzy. What's more, it's no myth that piranhas can strip all the meat off an animal in minutes. Farmers have reported seeing cattle disappear underwater, only to see a skeleton wash up on a bank within half an hour.

However, it *is* a myth that piranhas kill people. The idea of a person being eaten alive when he or she falls out of a boat or goes for a swim makes for gory movie material. But it simply does not happen. There is, in fact, no record of anyone ever having been killed by piranhas. Still, there are some cases of piranhas feeding on people who have drowned. Once in a while, human corpses somehow end up in the lakes and rivers where piranhas live, and piranhas will eat the corpses. These rare cases have fired the imaginations of many and led to the fantastic—and untrue— legends of killer piranhas.

Even so, the piranha can and does take good chunks out of humans from time to time. Its ability to smell blood is as keen as a shark's. And those who dangle hands and feet with cuts on them in piranha-infested waters may feel a sudden sharp pain. They may then find themselves missing a toe or finger.

"The piranha does not nibble or chew," explained a South American guide for the Amazon River. "It has teeth so sharp and jaws so strong that it can slice a piece of flesh from a man or an alligator as neatly as a razor. It can clip off a finger or toe, bone and all, with the ease of a meat cleaver."

Why, then, does the piranha take only a bite or two out of humans and move on? Why doesn't it devour us right down to the skeleton, as it devours other animals?

"It's quite possible that it just doesn't like us. Perhaps instinct makes it afraid of us," claimed the Amazon guide. "Luckily, when it comes to humans and piranhas, the feelings are mutual."

BITING THE HANDS THAT FEED THEM

Preview

For years, Sandra had lived happily with her pet chimpanzee, Travis. She cooked special meals for him, bought him clothing, and even taught him to drive. She treated this amazing, lovable chimp like her own son. Then, one day, a switch flipped in Travis's brain. Without warning, Sandra's pet suddenly turned into a furious, bloodthirsty monster.

BITING THE HANDS THAT FEED THEM

About 15,000 years ago, humans discovered something interesting about wolves. Even though adult wolves were dangerous and aggressive toward people, their pups were not. In fact, abandoned wolf pups raised by humans were remarkably tame and friendly. And as humans bred generation after generation of these wolves, the animals became downright lovable. Over time, most of the wild traits of the wolf disappeared. Replacing these traits were obedience and a desire to please. Humankind had its first pet—the dog.

Now it occurred to humans that if a wild creature could be turned into a companion, it should be possible to tame, or domesticate, other animals to use for food, fur, and labor. So, roughly 10,000 years ago, wild pigs, goats, sheep, and birds were domesticated. Five thousand years later, horses, donkeys, and camels followed. As recently as 2,800 years ago, we domesticated the wild turkey.

Somewhere between the domestication of pigs and chickens, wild cats began wandering into the growing settlements, looking for mice. Unlike wolves, these cats were less willing to be tamed. They remained somewhat solitary and suspicious. They were not particularly concerned about obeying or serving humans. Still, cats enjoyed the food and shelter people provided. And in time, cats began to put up with humans more and more, even showing affection when they felt like it. Humankind had found its second pet.

There was something very appealing about forcing the wildness out of animals. It made humans feel stronger and safer. In addition, pets made us feel needed and loved. Still, taming wild creatures was a hit-and-miss thing. It was baffling. Why did some birds need very little encouragement to sit on one's hand, while others refused to come within 100 yards of a person?

And what was it with zebras? Their close relative, the horse, had been moderately easy to tame and train. But the zebra would have nothing to do with humans. No amount of herding, chasing, or whipping could make a zebra back down. It would not be tamed.

Today, scientists understand that some creatures have certain genes that make them incapable of being entirely tamed. Regardless of what people do, a streak of wildness will remain. And sometimes this wildness is much wider than just a streak. Cats and dogs may actually prefer the comfort of a house and the company of their humans. However, many unusual or exotic animals that people attempt to force into friendship would prefer to be left in their natural homes. Sometimes the instincts of creatures forced into captivity take over. When this happens, the results can be disastrous—even deadly.

"Only a lunatic would walk into the midst of a pride of lions," wrote Edward Ricciutti, an author who studies animals and their attacks on humans. "Yet all over the United States, there are people who have taken lions and other wild cats into their homes. Many of these people know the danger involved but just do not care. Just like some people regularly drive while drunk and don't care."

Of the wild cats that people keep as pets, none is more popular (believe it or not) than the tiger. There are more than 5,000 tigers in homes across the United States. To get an idea of just how many tigers that is, there are *five times* more tigers in American homes than there are in zoos worldwide. In fact, the number of pet tigers is equal to the earth's entire tiger population living in the wild.

Many people look at these statistics and think, then, that raising a tiger is a good thing. After all, it helps rebuild the tiger's dwindling numbers. Also, many owners of wild cats believe that the love and kindness they show these creatures will be repaid. Somehow, they convince themselves that millions of years of evolution can be undone by a few years of petting, feeding, and protection.

"But savagery is part of a wild animal's nature, and it may surface at any time," Ricciutti added. "It is *right* for a lion, tiger, or leopard to be fierce. That is precisely how big cats should behave. They are supposed to be killers, not friends of man."

Every year this grim fact is reinforced over and over again.

In 2010, a 66-year-old Canadian man entered the pen where he kept a 650-pound Siberian tiger. In his hands, he held several pounds of meat for the tiger's meal. It was not a common practice for this man to enter the tiger's space, but perhaps he felt that he had reached a safe place with his "pet." After all, he truly believed that he had a special bond with this huge predator.

"He thought of his tiger like a family member," a neighbor commented. "He refused to believe that it was really dangerous."

Six years earlier, this same tiger had attacked and nearly killed a young boy who was visiting. The boy had been standing near the tiger, trying to take its picture. Perhaps he was too close to the tiger. Many wild animals have definite boundaries, and when strangers cross these boundaries, the animals get nervous. Or perhaps the tiger was not used to seeing children. Or maybe the tiger was just being a tiger. For whatever reason, the big cat jumped on the boy and tore at his face and neck. Luckily, the owner was able to get the tiger off the boy. The child was rushed to the hospital, where he later recovered.

Neighbors were horrified. They demanded that the laws in that part of Canada be changed, thereby making it illegal to keep such big, fierce animals as pets. The laws were changed, but the owner was so determined to keep his tiger that he hired a team of lawyers to fight back. Two years later, the new law was overturned, and the owner was reunited with his tiger. Then, three years later, the 66-year-old owner, for some reason, decided to personally deliver lunch face-to-face with his tiger.

"No one else was there, so we don't really know what happened," authorities later reported.

The tiger's owner was found dead and torn to bits. Not ten feet away, the pet tiger was calmly cleaning his bloody paws. He stared curiously at the policemen standing nervously just outside his rickety cage.

"Why anyone would want to keep a monkey is beyond me," Ricciuti wrote in his book *Killer Animals*. "It is like sharing one's home with a dirty, nasty, and thoroughly uncontrollable human being."

Still, monkeys are astonishingly popular pets in the United States. It is estimated that there are close to 20,000 primates in homes across the country. The fascination with monkeys is obvious. They look more like human beings than any other animal. They're very intelligent, and under the right circumstances, they can be quite affectionate and well-trained.

"People see monkeys on TV, at the zoo, in a circus," said a zookeeper in San Diego. "Monkeys are always presented as sort of funny and harmless children. And so we begin to think of monkeys as little humans. They can look you in the eye, laugh, and shake your hand. Who wouldn't want a pet like that? And that's the danger, because monkeys are wild animals. Some have terrific tempers. And nearly all of them, like any wild animal, are unpredictable."

Many monkeys that are bred as pets are taken away from their mothers when they are far too young to be separated. This is done intentionally so that the baby monkey will bond with humans instead of monkeys. However, this practice has proven to be a huge mistake. Young monkeys suffer anxiety, depression, and anger. They often develop strange habits like biting themselves and walking in circles. These emotional problems usually worsen when a monkey is placed in a house with humans.

"If you try to keep monkeys as pets, you're creating a mentally disturbed animal in 99.9 percent of the cases," said veterinarian Kevin Wright, a director at the Phoenix Zoo in Arizona. "The animal will never be able to fit in anywhere. It will never learn how to get along with other monkeys. And, more often than not, it will end up with a lot more traits that are self-destructive."

But it's hard to convince those who are dead-set on owning a monkey that it is a bad idea. A baby monkey looks completely harmless. It's small and furry with huge eyes, like a stuffed toy. And it looks adorable when it holds and drinks from a bottle, just like a human baby. In fact, it is this tendency to think of a baby monkey as a "replacement" for a child that often leads to monkey ownership.

"We're looking for a baby monkey to love and spoil," wrote a woman from Orlando, Florida, on a website for exotic pet adoption. "We are unable to have any more children and have a void in our hearts. We need a baby to love!"

As many of these owners soon find out, the cuddly baby quickly becomes a restless and moody 150-pound animal that requires an immense amount of attention and care. Unlike a child, it never grows up and cannot completely take care of itself.

It was this longing to fill a void that led Sandra Herold to think of her pet chimpanzee, Travis, as her son. Sandra's daughter, an only child, had died suddenly in a car accident. Understandably heartbroken, Sandra devoted all her energy and affection to the family's chimp. Unlike many pet monkeys across the country, Travis was by no means neglected once he became a 200-pound adult. He often accompanied Sandra Herold when she went into town. He held her hand

and followed orders with a nod. He posed for pictures, flashing a big goofy smile and waving at photographers. At night, Sandra cooked steak and crab legs for her "son."

As the years passed, Travis became something of a celebrity. He learned to dress himself, use the bathroom, shake hands, and even drink wine from a crystal goblet. He watched television, using a remote control, and watered plants when prompted to do so by Sandra. On two occasions, he drove a car around the farm Sandra owned. Many of these skills astounded friends and neighbors, but as one primate expert pointed out, "Chimps are incredibly smart. Given enough attention and training, none of these accomplishments are that unusual—even driving a car."

And Travis was so well-behaved that one friend joked that the chimp was more obedient than his own children. This intelligence and obedience led Travis to star in commercials for Coca-Cola and Old Navy. He even made appearances in movies and television shows. But beneath the clothes, the trained smile, and the formal handshakes, Travis was still an animal. There was still a mysterious wildness in him that could not be erased, no matter how much he acted like a human. And one day, that wildness exploded.

"Help! Send the police! He's killing my friend!" Sandra Herold screamed on the phone to a 911 operator.

"Who's killing your friend?" the operator asked.

"Hurry! Tell them to bring guns!" Sandra shouted in panic.

"Guns? Who has guns?"

"No, no! Please! Tell the police to bring guns. They have to shoot him!" Sandra pleaded through tears.

"Who?" The operator asked again. "Who's hurting your friend?"

"My chimpanzee! Oh my God. He's torn her face off!"

In a sudden and unexplained fit of rage, Travis had attacked Sandra's best friend, Charla Nash. Travis had seen Charla hundreds of times and knew her well. But on a February morning in 2009, a switch in his brain seemed to flip. Travis became furious and determined to kill Charla. In the driveway of Sandra's home, he used his sharp canine teeth to rip off Charla's nose, lips, and most of her jaw. He clawed her eyes out and then chewed off both her hands.

"She's dead! Oh my God. Now he's eating her!" Sandra screamed.

Then Travis came after his owner, his sharp

teeth bared. Sandra rushed into her house, where she grabbed a butcher knife and stabbed the raging chimp. Only slightly wounded, Travis dashed back outside, where police cars now surrounded the house.

"He knows how to open car doors!" Sandra shrieked in warning as Travis bounded toward a cruiser. In a flash, the 14-year-old monkey opened a back door and reached for the officer. Three gunshots rang out. Travis was dead.

Charla Nash was not killed, but she suffered horrific injuries that left her face terribly disfigured. Sandra Herold suffered injuries of a different kind.

"I'm hollow now," she said after Travis's death. "I have nothing left." One year later, Sandra died of natural causes. Many felt she had died of a broken heart.

In 2004, a truly gruesome and nightmarish story appeared in newspapers around the world. It might be the ultimate exotic-pet-turned-killer tale. According to the story, neighbors of 30-year-old Mark Voegel of Germany began complaining about a bad odor coming from Voegel's apartment. When police officers finally got inside Voegel's apartment, they were met with an unbelievable sight.

"It was like a horror movie," a police spokes-person reportedly said. "His corpse was over the sofa. Giant webs draped him, and spiders were all over him. They were coming out of his nose and his mouth."

According to the newspaper story, Voegel was a collector of hundreds of dangerous reptiles, spiders, and insects. He was a loner who rarely invited anyone over to his apartment. However, on occasion, acquaintances had seen what Voegel referred to as his "jungle home."

"He had some very aggressive spiders and snakes—the kinds of things no one should ever have in a home," one visitor to the apartment said. "He allowed many of the non-poisonous reptiles to roam free. And he didn't seem to really have any fear of the poisonous spiders and snakes."

The police report claimed that Voegel had been bitten by one of his black widows, had not sought treatment, and had died about two weeks before his body was discovered. During those two weeks, heating elements on many of the cages had supposedly exploded and displaced the tops of the cages. This allowed all of Voegel's creepy creatures to roam free. Rumors soon spread about police reports that were full of ghastly details.

"Larger pieces of flesh torn off by the lizards were scooped up and taken back to the webs of tarantulas and other bird-eating spiders," claimed one report.

"One tarantula had built a nest the size of a swallow's nest in the corner of the ceiling. Thousands of termites had eaten away most of Voegel's flesh," claimed another.

Not long after this story surfaced, readers began questioning it. A number of details just didn't add up. For one thing, it is very unlikely that a grown man would die from a black widow bite. Voegel may have been sick for several days, but he probably would not have died. And termites eating his body? That would be pretty unusual, since termites eat only plant matter, not flesh.

Still, this story produced nightmares. The idea of dangerous pets turning on their owners in such a grisly way made people's skin crawl. Whether or not this story was entirely (or even partly) true, it had an impact.

"I don't quite buy that whole tale," said an entomologist (a person who studies insects) in Germany. "The entire thing may be a lie. But if it keeps just one person from thinking that it would be fun to keep dangerous creatures in his or her home, it was worth the lie. Some things are just better left in the wild."

LIONS CLOSE TO HOME

Preview

Cindy Parolin has tackled a mountain lion that was attacking her son. Her son has escaped, but now Cindy is pinned on top of the lion, staring deep into its angry eyes. One false move or a quick look away could mean death. "Go get help," Cindy whispers to her children. But help is hard to find. And night is closing in.

LIONS CLOSE TO HOME

**Warning! Mountain Lions in This Area!
Be Alert—Watch Children Closely!**

Cindy Parolin had often seen these signs posted near trails and roads. She and her family lived in an area of British Columbia, Canada, where many mountain lions roamed. However, Cindy was not too worried. Mountain lions, also known as cougars or pumas, were pretty shy animals. They usually preferred to stay as far from humans as possible. In all of her 36 years, Cindy had seen mountain lions only a few times, at a distance.

Still, Cindy glanced back at her three children, who were riding on horseback behind her. Eleven-year-old Melissa hummed a tune and gazed at the sky. Thirteen-year-old David sat up tall, holding the reins like a pro. And six-year-old Steven appeared to be chattering to his old horse, Goomba, who trotted along, listening patiently. Cindy's fourth child, nine-year-old Billy, had chosen to go with their father to help set up the camp. The two had driven there earlier in the day, while Cindy and the other children had ridden horses along the same road. It was a rarely used road, driven mostly by campers and hikers. The Parolins' camp was now only a few miles away.

"What's for dinner? I'm starved!" shouted Steven.

"We'll have to see what your dad has whipped up," Cindy answered with a grin. No matter what was happening, her youngest son was always hungry and thinking about food. Steven was small for his age, but full of energy. Briefly, Cindy frowned as she recalled a mountain lion attack on a small boy about Steven's age. It had happened very recently. And it had taken place on Vancouver Island, also in British Columbia.

People who lived on Vancouver Island were proud of their mountain lion population.

Nowhere on earth were so many cougars concentrated in one area. Most of the people who lived there rarely saw the lions. The big cats usually stayed up in the mountains and kept to themselves. Even so, there were plenty of stories about the cougars. Some were funny. One time a cougar was spotted on someone's roof chasing a weathervane in circles, trying to catch the little metal bird. Another time, a cougar wandered into the parking garage of the island's fanciest hotel.

"Get to your cars! Lion on the loose!" the garage attendant had bellowed frantically at guests returning to their cars after dinner at the hotel's popular restaurant. Men in silk suits and women in heels looked blankly at the attendant.

"What?" laughed a man. "Cougars don't hang out in garages. What have you been drinking, dude?"

At that very moment, the big cat strolled out from a dark corner and yawned widely. Never before had guests run so quickly through that garage.

Other times, the mountain lion stories were not funny at all.

On a cool spring morning, seven-year-old Kyle Musselman was walking to school with his older brother and sister. The three siblings had to walk down a long hillside staircase that was closely surrounded by trees and bushes. As always, Kyle wanted to race to the bottom of the stairs.

"Come on!" he shouted. As he bounded down the stairs, he giggled and hooted. Suddenly, a dark shape seemed to appear out of nowhere. It was flying through the air, wide paws extended. It landed on Kyle's back and threw him to the ground.

"Damn!" Kyle's older brother said in horror. "It's a cougar! Somebody . . . help!"

The mountain lion was already trying to bite Kyle around the neck, searching for the main artery to slash with its sharp canine teeth. But this little human was not like its normal prey. The neck was nothing like a deer's. It was far too short. In frustration, the mountain lion began biting at Kyle's head and face. Kyle screamed shrilly over and over again as he beat the cougar with his small hands. Neighbors came running as shouts of "Cougar!" rang up and down the street.

Within minutes, Kyle's father was tearing down the stairs toward his son. Now the mountain lion was trying to drag Kyle away and into the thick woods.

"No!" his father shouted furiously at the lion. "Get off him!"

The lion stared straight at Kyle's father and

held his gaze. But he would not drop Kyle, whose head now hung limply, covered in blood.

"Damn you!" Kyle's father roared as he ran toward the mountain lion. "I said, GET OFF HIM!"

Without a second thought for his own safety, Kyle's father threw himself at the lion. Surprised, the lion finally released Kyle and disappeared in a blur into the woods. Kyle was sprawled facedown. He was motionless, and blood was spreading around him. His father gently turned him over. The face that met him was no longer his youngest son's. Kyle's cheeks and forehead were like raw hamburger meat. Flaps of skin hung off his skull, and a deflated eyeball had fallen out of its socket. Some of the bites were so severe that Kyle's father could see into his son's nasal cavity. He was sure he was dead.

Then there was a gurgling moan. A bloody air bubble formed where Kyle's lips had been.

"Hey buddy," his father said quietly, fighting his tears. "It's Dad. Are you OK?"

After a long pause, Kyle mumbled, "No. No, Dad."

It would take 14 hours of surgery, but Kyle's face was wired, stitched, and pieced back together. He would never look like the same laughing little kid he had been, but he would live.

"I can't tell you how lucky you are to have your son still alive," the young female surgeon said to Kyle's parents the next day. "He's little, but he's a fighter."

However, as Cindy Parolin rode along on horseback with her children on that warm summer afternoon, she thought of cougars only briefly. Cindy was a strong, fearless woman. She knew both the hazards and the joys of traveling deep into the Canadian wilderness. And, more than anything, she respected the awesome nature that surrounded her. Though she was an expert hunter who knew how to handle both a rifle and a knife, she preferred to coexist peacefully with wild animals. She knew that mountain lions, on very rare occasions, were a threat. But she was glad that they now thrived in Canada. Only thirty years earlier, these beautiful creatures had been endangered.

"Almost there!" Cindy called back to her kids. And it was a good thing. The ride had taken longer than she had expected, and now the sun was beginning to dip into the trees. Birds were making their evening sounds, and across a wide valley came the yips of coyotes preparing to hunt. It would feel good to get off the horses and stretch. And it seemed to Cindy that her horse was either tired or irritated. He kept jerking and jumping as he trotted along.

Cindy turned around to see how the other horses were doing. She was surprised to see that the other three appeared uneasy, too. Steven's horse, Goomba, had flattened his ears, and his eyes darted around. David's horse was doing a weird, jerky prance. And then Cindy saw it. Something was running behind the trees, keeping pace with the horses. It stayed low to the ground, making absolutely no sound. Then it disappeared. Cindy strained her eyes in the fading light. Perhaps it had only been a deer.

But deer don't chase horses, Cindy was thinking at the very moment a streak of gold exploded out of the trees. Mountain lion! The lion's wide paws were stretched as it landed on top of Goomba. But Goomba reared and shifted away before the cougar could get a firm grip. In its panic, the old horse had thrown little Steven to the ground. As Goomba ran off, Cindy and her two other children quickly hopped off their horses and let the terrified animals also run ahead. Now the cougar stood directly in front of Steven. For several seconds the cat and the boy stared hard at each other.

"Stevie, don't . . ." Cindy began.

But it was too late. Steven turned to run. Like any cat, the mountain lion cannot resist a chase.

It was most likely why Kyle Musselman had been attacked. It was why a cougar was found running in circles on a rooftop after a weathervane. And it was why this mountain lion had leaped at Goomba—not for food, but for the thrill of chase and capture. And now its target was Steven.

Steven was thrown facedown. The cat then proceeded to bite the little boy's scalp, making long tears and rips. Instantly, Cindy grabbed a four-foot stick and ran, screaming, at the lion. She jabbed at the lion's face and whacked him repeatedly with the heavy stick. But the mountain lion completely ignored Cindy and held on to Steven. Then Cindy did something remarkably brave.

"No!" she shouted as she threw herself on top of the cat and rolled it over on its back. Surprised, the lion released Steven. In a flash, Cindy jammed her arm into the lion's mouth. Now, as Cindy lay sprawled on top of the cat, it remained motionless except for its swishing tail. Its dark green eyes narrowed and stared fiercely into Cindy's eyes. Cindy stared right back.

"Mom," David whispered shakily. "What should we do?"

Huddled close to David were Melissa and Steven. Steven was bleeding terribly, but luckily the lion had not touched his face. Still, his scalp was in tatters.

"Go get your father," Cindy said quietly, never breaking eye contact with the lion. "Get help for Steven."

Camp was not far away, but Steven had to be helped along slowly. His loss of blood was beginning to make him weak. In spite of his pain, Steven glanced up at his older sister and gave a half-hearted grin.

"Does it look really bad?" he asked hopefully.

"Yeah, it's pretty gross," Melissa said truthfully.

"Mom will be all right, won't she?" Steven asked.

There was a long silence, and then Melissa answered not quite as truthfully, "Sure. She'll be fine."

It would take nearly an hour for help to reach Cindy Parolin. Even though the three Parolin children found their father's car, they couldn't find the campsite he and their older brother had set up.

"Dad! Billy! Help!"

Melissa and David's voices rang through the woods. The sun was quite low now, and both children were worried that darkness would make their mother's and their little brother's situations even more dangerous.

"HELP!"

Not far away, friends of the Parolins, Jim and Karen Manion, sat at their own camp. Jim recognized the voices at once. Immediately, Jim and Karen ran toward the shouts. David explained frantically that their mother was back down the road with a cougar pinned beneath her. Jim didn't ask any questions. He grabbed his shotgun, whistled for his dog, and ran to his truck.

"Come with me, David," he ordered. "Karen will take care of Melissa and Steven. They'll find your father. I need you to lead me to your mother."

What could possibly have been going through Cindy Parolin's mind as she lay there in the dimming light, one arm gripping a mountain lion's neck and the other arm jammed in its mouth? Perhaps she worried about her children. Perhaps she thought of nothing but survival. Maybe quick panicked thoughts of other cougar attacks crossed her mind. After all, a woman her age had been attacked and killed while out running in the hills near Sacramento, California, only a year earlier.

At just a little over 100 pounds, mountain lions are not that big, but they are amazingly strong. "Cougars can easily bring down prey four times their size," newspapers announced after the attack in California. "A small woman is no match for a full-grown cougar."

Perhaps Cindy thought of this as she struggled to hold down the lion. She was barely 5 foot 2 and weighed less than 120 pounds.

"Cindy! Where are you?"

"Mom! We're here!"

David had led Jim Manion back to the right spot. A flurry of horse prints covered the dirt road. And splatters of blood dotted the dust. But there was no sign of Cindy. Jim worried that the cougar may have dragged Cindy into the woods. Then an eerily calm voice drifted from behind some trees.

"I'm over here."

Jim stared into the dark trees. Cindy's voice came from not more than 20 yards away.

"Cindy, is the cat still nearby?" Jim asked quietly.

"Yes. It is here with me," came the steady reply.

Jim turned to David, whose face had gone white, and told him to return to the truck and stay there. Meanwhile, Jim cocked his weapon. His hands shook so much that he could barely keep a grip on the gun. If only he could see Cindy and the lion, he would feel better. Then Jim noticed something that gave him hope. Near the edge of the trees was Cindy's leather jacket. It looked as though she had taken it off and even folded it. Perhaps she was still in control of the cat.

Then Jim crept around a large tree, and his hope sank. Cindy lay flat on her back only twenty yards or so away. She was covered in dirt and blood, and the sharp smell of blood filled the still air. Resting a flexed paw on Cindy's shoulder, with its face only inches from hers, was the lion. It was staring straight at Jim. Jim ducked behind the tree and took a deep breath. There was no way he could take a shot at the cougar while it was right on top of Cindy. Instead, he carefully picked up some rocks.

"Cindy, your children are all OK," Jim said in a low voice. "You'll be OK, too."

There was a long pause, and then Cindy said, as calmly as before, "I'm dying."

There was not a second to spare. Jim stood up and shouted at the lion. He threw rocks and stomped—anything to get the cougar to move so that he could get a clear shot at it. But the lion never flinched. In desperation, Jim shot into the air. Still, the lion remained utterly motionless, staring straight at Jim.

What kind of animal is this!? Jim wondered in fear and frustration. In all his years of hiking, hunting, and camping, he had never seen a creature sit still at the sound of a gun. Finally, Jim made a tough decision.

"David, let the dog out!" Jim called back in the direction of the truck. Jim knew that the cougar would likely kill his faithful old hunting dog, but he had no other choice. The dog came dashing out and went straight toward the lion and began running circles around it. Naturally, the cougar could not resist the chase. The two charged away, wrestling briefly in the woods, and then they both ran back toward Jim. To Jim's amazement, his dog had not been injured, and now it rushed to Jim's side, looking at him obediently.

The cougar stopped short of Jim, crouched low and prepared to attack. Jim aimed, pulled the trigger, and . . . the gun jammed! The lion continued to stare as Jim began backing very slowly toward the truck while re-cocking the shotgun. At that very moment, another truck appeared on the roadway. The curious driver stopped to see what was going on and got out of his vehicle.

"Watch out! Cougar!" Jim shouted.

The stranger jumped right back in his truck and slammed the door.

Finally, the mountain lion had had enough. There was just too much activity going on.

It stretched casually and began strolling right down the middle of the road as if to show how completely fearless it was. Jim's gun finally unjammed, and he blasted a shot in the direction of the lion. Again, the cougar barely flinched. It turned around to give one last parting stare. Then it slowly disappeared into the woods.

"That was the strangest animal," Jim would later say. "I will never figure it out."

Sadly, Cindy Parolin's last words to Jim were true. She had lost too much blood, and on the way to the hospital, she died. She had made a parent's greatest sacrifice, giving her own life to save her son's. Little Steven would need some stitches, but his wounds would heal completely.

The Parolin children all decided to wait until they were older to hear the details of what Jim Manion saw on that evening in 1996. Perhaps Jim kindly omitted some of the more gruesome details. But he told the story of the mysterious lion. And, to this day, an odd piece of the puzzle remains the biggest mystery of all. How did Cindy's jacket end up several yards away from her, neatly folded? Except for a few fang punctures, the jacket was clean and mostly free of blood.

The most agreed-upon answer is that Cindy Parolin had almost escaped unharmed. When two lions fight, the winner pins the loser on its back and stares into its eyes. This is exactly what Cindy had done. Normally, the defeated lion gives up and retreats, knowing that the stronger lion could kill it. Perhaps that evening, when Cindy loosened her grip on the lion, it had freed itself from beneath her and run back into the dark woods. Perhaps, then, Cindy had taken off the jacket to check her arm. Out of habit, she folded it and set it down. Then, hearing a rustling in the woods, perhaps Cindy's terror took over. Maybe she began walking quickly, or maybe she broke into a fast run toward safety.

If this is what happened, it was a fatal error. It was likely that the curious cat was still lurking nearby. It heard the rush of feet and saw a blur of motion. It crouched, and then it sprang. And this time, it landed on top.

In the end, as always, the lion simply could not resist the chase.

THE DEADLIEST CREATURE OF ALL

Preview

Finally, we meet the most deadly animal on Earth. No other creature comes close in its ability to kill human beings. At the same time, this animal is unmatched at saving human lives. What could this creature be?

THE DEADLIEST CREATURE OF ALL

There is still one animal on our planet that is far more dangerous—to both humans and other animals—than any other creature discussed in this book. Like a lion or tiger, it is a skilled hunter. However, it often hunts simply for the thrill of the kill, not because it is hungry. Its ability to watch, wait, and attack with startling swiftness completely outdoes the crocodile's. Like the grizzly, it will often do anything to protect its young. And its unexpected outbursts of deadly temper are far more common than a monkey's.

But it is this creature's unique traits that make it the deadliest. No other animal actually plots and plans the death of humans, but this one does. No other animal kills out of jealousy, pride, love, revenge, or frustration, but this one does—quite often. And no other animal reflects on its actions after killing a human, sometimes bragging and sometimes crying. But this one does. The animal? Obviously, it is man.

Compared to the other creatures in this book, we humans seem poorly equipped to kill one another. We possess no dangerous poison or sharp stingers. We're not really that big, and we can't run very fast. We have rather dull nails instead of claws, and our mouths are totally fang-free. However, we have one thing that makes us superior to other creatures—our brains. Because we are, by a long shot, the most intelligent creatures on earth, we are considered civilized and advanced. We have invented many things that make living easier and make our lives last longer. But humans have also invented things that make our lives shorter: weapons.

To be fair, weapons are not unique to humans. For example, elephants have been seen throwing rocks at people. In 2009, a Korean woman was knocked unconscious when two elephants at a zoo intentionally threw fist-sized rocks at her.

"They seemed angry about something," a bystander said. "Then they sized this woman up and picked up rocks in their trunks. They were definitely aiming at her head. They knew what they were doing."

When the woman finally opened her eyes, the two elephants were standing near the edge of the fence staring at her and—quite possibly in anger—stamping their feet.

In 2007, apes were observed, for the first time, using weapons against humans. In an area of the Congo, gorillas have long been seen using sticks to measure the depth of water. If the stick goes in too far, the gorillas choose a different place to crossing the river or lake. Scientists were amazed to discover that apes knew how to use a stick as a measuring tool. But recently, these same gorillas demonstrated their understanding of other uses for sticks.

"It began as a rock-throwing fight," a scientist explained. "A local man was tossing pebbles at the gorillas to see what they would do. What they did was really not that surprising. They picked up the pebbles and threw them right back at the man, mimicking his actions."

What happened next, however, was surprising. As the tempers of the gorillas flared, they grabbed sticks and hurled them at the man. Some of the more aggressive gorillas were seen waving large sticks angrily, holding them like clubs. They were using weapons. It was an obvious threat.

"It was frightening," the scientist concluded. "It was nearly human."

Perhaps the apes' actions looked human, but human weapons are far more deadly and advanced than large sticks. Some weapons are intended for hunting or protection against dangerous animals. However, most of our weapons were created to destroy either humans or the areas where humans live. And these weapons are quite effective.

How good are we at killing one another? In 2007, it was estimated that, worldwide, murder took 520,000 lives. Various wars took 310,000, suicide took another 815,000, and law-enforcement killings took 14,000 lives. A total of 1,659,000 lives were lost through human-against-human violence. During wars, these numbers have skyrocketed. In the United States, 620,000 people died during the Civil War. And World War II saw the deaths of 60 million people. Nearly 6 million of these were victims of the Holocaust, one of humankind's most monstrous examples of violence.

In comparison, the much-feared shark kills about 12 people worldwide a year. Only 107 people have been killed by bears—in the past *one hundred years!* And no one has been killed by a black widow spider in the United States in the past three years. Perhaps these dangerous creatures do not seem so dangerous after all when placed alongside human beings.

Besides, violence is not the only method we use to kill one another. In fact, violent deaths are only a fraction of the total deaths caused by humans. It may be true that mosquitoes (the deadliest creature, other than man, on earth) are responsible for killing two million people a year by spreading malaria. But people are much more successful at infecting one another with deadly diseases. Worldwide, more than 15 million people a year die from contagious diseases. The common cold, flu, and AIDS/HIV are all spread through human contact, and these three diseases take millions of lives. AIDS and HIV-related diseases alone account for nearly two million deaths a year.

Still, humans are not alone in their ability to kill one another with violence and disease. Many animals wage what might be seen as war against each other. Male lions that want to take over a pride will attack the current male leader of the pride and then kill all his offspring. Ants in search of food or territory will organize and attack entire colonies. One species of ants fights so often that it is known as the army ant. Army ants have been known to stage sneak attacks and use tactics like trapping and drowning. And some chimpanzees have been observed hunting down other groups of chimps and killing them—just to show their superior strength.

However, humans reign supreme in one area.

"Our most effective method of killing each other will probably turn out to be the destruction of our environment," writes Gordon Grice, the author of a book about killer animals titled *Deadly Kingdom*.

Seven billion humans now live on planet Earth. Not long ago, scientists estimated that our world could handle no more than five billion people before it began dying from pollution, overcrowding, and overuse. Today, traces of prescription drugs are found in our rivers. Choking smog often forces people to hide inside their homes. Holes have been punched in the ozone layer as a result of chemicals in the air. Great sections of polar icecaps are melting, possibly creating major changes in the weather.

"How long do we have?" asked one scientist. "It's difficult to say. But it isn't difficult to realize that man is man's greatest threat."

Fearsome animals live in every corner of the earth. As the title of this book points out, some of these animals are creatures that can kill you. But it should be noted that "can kill you" is very different from "will kill you." Nearly all of the dangerous animals presented in this book would much prefer to avoid humans altogether. With the possible exception of the crocodile, most animals do not hunt humans. Even the meat-eaters don't seem to really like human flesh. Some experts claim that this is because humans contain too much fat and not enough protein.

But others claim that it is instinct that keeps predators from hunting humans.

"Millions of years have taught animals to fear man," one writer said. "For all the claws and teeth and power and wildness of the creatures that roam this earth, there are no animals as terrifying as the human being."

Sometimes our fear of 800-pound bears, hissing cobras, or screaming ants makes us forget that they are not necessarily dangerous. They are not looking for a fight or a victim. In most cases, they are as afraid of us as we are of them. However, if cornered or threatened by something as scary as a human being, many creatures will react with violence. They will use the weapons they have to get rid of us, just as we would use our weapons to get rid of them. In the end, the fear response of a human is not much different from that of a brainless sea wasp. Each will do what it has to do to survive.

"Life is as dear to all creatures as it is to man," said the Dalai Lama, the spiritual leader of Tibet. "Just as we want happiness and fear pain, just as we want to live and not die, so do all other creatures."